# REDISCOVERED EARLY CHURCH
# PreMillennialism
*Teachings of the Earliest Church Fathers on Prophecy*

## by *Robert Franklin*

REDISCOVERED EARLY CHURCH

# PreMillennialism

*Teachings of the Earliest Church Fathers on Prophecy*

ROBERT FRANKLIN, D.Min.
WORD LAMP PUBLICATIONS, LLC.
ARLINGTON, TEXAS

**Rediscovered Early Church Premillennialism:**
Teachings of the Earliest Church Fathers on Prophecy

All Scripture quotations unless otherwise indicated are taken from the (NASB) NEW AMERICAN STANDARD BIBLE®, Copyright © 1960,1962,1963,1968,1971,1972,1973,1975,1977,1995 by The Lockman Foundation. Used by permission.

Scripture quotations marked (NIV) are taken from the Holy Bible, NEW INTERNATIONAL VERSION®, NIV® Copyright © 1973, 1978, 1984, 2011 by Biblica, Inc.® Used by permission. All rights reserved worldwide.

Scripture quotations marked (NIrV) are taken from the Holy Bible, NEW INTERNATIONAL READER'S VERSION®. Copyright © 1996, 1998 Biblica. All rights reserved throughout the world. Used by permission of Biblica.

Scripture quotations marked (NCV) are taken from the Holy Bible the New Century Version®. Copyright © 2005 by Thomas Nelson, Inc. Used by permission. All rights reserved.

Scripture quotations marked (NLT) are taken from the Holy Bible, New Living Translation, copyright © 1996, 2004, 2007 by Tyndale House Foundation. Used by permission of Tyndale House Publishers, Inc., Carol Stream, Illinois 60188. All rights reserved.

Scripture quotations marked (ESV) are taken from The ESV® Bible (The Holy Bible, English Standard Version®) copyright © 2001 by Crossway, a publishing ministry of Good News Publishers. Used by permission. All rights reserved.

Scripture quotations marked (GNT) are from the Holy Bible, Good News Translation®, Copyright © 1992 American Bible Society. Used by permission. All rights reserved.

Scripture quotations marked (NKJV) are from the Holy Bible the New King James Version®. Copyright © 1982 by Thomas Nelson, Inc. Used by permission. All rights reserved.

**Library of Congress Cataloging-in-Publication Data**
Franklin, Robert H.
Rediscovered Early Church Premillennialism: Teachings of the Earliest Church Fathers on Prophecy – 1st ed.  p. cm.

ISBN-10:1938239059; ISBN-13: 978-1-938239-05-2 (Trade Paper Edition)
ISBN-10:1938239067; ISBN-13: 978-1-938239-06-9 (EPUB)
ISBN-10: 1938239075; ISBN-13: 978-1-938239-076 (Kindle)

1. Prophecy — Eschatology — Spirituality — Christianity 2. Non-Fiction 3. Thought and Thinking — Religious Aspects I. Title.
Includes bibliographical references.
Printed in the United States of America
Printed by Createspace
Cover Design, Editing and Interior Design by Susan Franklin using Adobe Indesign;
Visit Susan at: ElegantBookDesign@gmail.com
Published by: Word Lamp Publications LLC, P.O. Box 181257, Arlington, Texas 76096
12 11 10 9 8 7 6 5 4 3 2 1

# CONTENTS

# INTRODUCTION

Lena must have shivered as one chilled from shock. Even while the sweet aroma of Christmas baking wafted through the house and out to the snowy scene outside, a sadness filled her soul. Her wedding ring was missing.

On that Christmas in Sweden the family looked everywhere. Later, they even had their kitchen floor pulled up in hopes of finding the ring, to no avail. The ring was lost.

Sixteen summers and winters passed. Lena gave up hope of ever finding her wedding ring.

One day, while picking produce from her garden, she pulled up a small carrot and there—wrapped around the head of the carrot—was her wedding ring. The carrot had sprouted in the middle of the ring. It was the surprise of her life!

Perhaps the ring had slid off her fingers in vegetable peelings that became compost, she thought. However the ring was lost, its rediscovery was incredible. Sixteen years removed from the day of Christmas baking, she was holding her white gold band with its seven small diamonds. Her lost wedding ring had been rediscovered![1]

After the first three centuries of the Christian faith, another treasure was also lost.

This treasure was the premillennial view of prophecy taught by the earliest church fathers, who are known in theological circles as the Ante-Nicene fathers. They ministered "Ante," prefix meaning "before," the First Nicene Council of the Christian Church in AD 325. The majority of these earliest fathers of the church interpreted Scripture to teach that Jesus Christ will return before *(pre)* the millennium, an interpretation of Bible prophecy called premillennialism. Dr. Lewis Sperry Chafer, first President of Dallas Theological Seminary, confirms:

7

> Premillennialism was the all-but-universal belief of the early church. . . . It has been conceded that it was "**lost**," along with other vital truths, at the end of the third century and remained hidden until the Reformation. . . . The Reformers did **not** restore all features of [early church premillennial] doctrine.[2]

It is generally held that historic premillennialism, compiled during the sixteenth century, restated early church premillennialism. However, religious wars during the Reformation (1517–1648) hindered minority Reformers from thoroughly researching early church writings archived in Catholic and even Protestant churches. Consequently, "the Reformers did not restore all features of [early church premillennial] doctrine."[3]

As a result, the earliest church fathers' premillennial teachings on Scriptural prophecy remained lost.

In the nineteenth century, a new version of premillennialism, pretribulational dispensational premillennialism, was introduced by John Nelson Darby. Although many Christians today assume that this eschatological version mirrors the premillennial teachings of the early church, it does not, as a leading dispensationalist, Dr. Larry Crutchfield, remarks:

> John Nelson Darby, for example, undercut the patristic precedent for his own eschatological views by summarily **dismissing** the mass of the primitive [early church] fathers.[4]

With Darby's dismissal of even the earliest church fathers' writings on premillennialism, the pretribulational dispensational premillennial view of prophecy widely held today is not the premillennialism of the early church. Consequently, the earliest church fathers' premillennial teachings on Scriptural prophecy remained lost.

A resource available today which did not exist when modern interpretations of prophecy were documented is the exhaustive ten-volume collection entitled *The Ante-Nicene Fathers, Translations of the Writings of the Fathers Down to A.D. 325*. First translated in English in 1867, the preface of the 1885 reprint states that "no Christian scholar has ever before possessed in faithful versions of such compact form a supplement so essential to the right understanding of the New Testament itself. It is a volume indispensable to all scholars, and to every library, private or public."[5] Now available online, this ten-volume collection of early church writings, *The Ante-Nicene Fathers, Translations of the Writings of the Fathers Down to A.D. 325*, has made possible the rediscovery of early church premillennialism.

Like the lost wedding ring rediscovered after sixteen years, the early church premillennial view of prophecy has been rediscovered after seventeen centuries.

In *Rediscovered Early Church Premillennialism: Teachings of the Earliest Church Fathers on Prophecy*, you will find almost a hundred quotations from Ante-Nicene fathers and a logical sequence of end time events that corresponds to biblical and early church teachings.

So, who were the early church Ante-Nicene fathers, and why should we listen to them today?

# 1

# THE ANTE-NICENE FATHERS

Not surprisingly, a "Top 100" ranking of the most influential people in history does not list even one Ante-Nicene father. So who were they?

Ante-Nicene fathers were leading ministers of the early church. They served as bishops, apologists (defenders of the faith), evangelists, theologians, and writers. They served during the era which extended from the first century to the First Nicene Council of the Christian Church in AD 325.

Since the period of the church fathers extends from the first to the eighth century, in this book the Ante-Nicene fathers are referred to as the earliest church fathers. Having discussed who they were, should they be called fathers and why should we listen to them today?

## SHOULD THEY BE CALLED "FATHERS"?

At first the term "fathers" might appear to conflict with the words of Jesus who said, "Do not call anyone on earth 'father,' for you have one Father, and he is in heaven" (Matthew 23:9 NIV). But in context Jesus was not addressing the parental relationship. Rather, He was contrasting the haughtiness of the Pharisees with the humility that Christ expects of His followers. The Pharisees desired status, recognition, and pretentious titles to impress people. Their attitude was one of pride. In contrast, Jesus taught His followers to serve humbly, saying, "The greatest among you will be your servant" (Matthew 23:11 NIV).

If an ecclesiastical title "father" was intended to impress, this would not be consistent with servant leadership. But such was not the case with the term "fathers" given to the Ante-Nicene fathers.

One reason why the Ante-Nicene fathers were called "fathers" stems from apostle Paul's letter to his converts in Corinth: "If you were to have countless tutors in Christ, yet you would not have many **fathers**, for in Christ Jesus I became your **father** through the gospel" (1 Corinthians 4:14-15). As founder of the Corinthian church, "Paul had been their spiritual father in that he gave them the gospel and helped to lead them to Christ."[1]

You may not recognize the name Agnes Bojaxhiu (1910–1997), who founded the Missionaries of Charity in Calcutta, India. But after forty-five years her humanitarian work grew to 610 missions in more than 123 countries, earning her the Nobel Peace Prize. To the poor, the orphans, the sick, and the dying of Calcutta, she was affectionately known as "Mother" Teresa.

Just as Agnes Bojaxhiu came to be known by those to whom she served as Mother, and just as Paul came to be known by Corinthian believers as their spiritual father, so the Christian teachers and pastors during the Ante-Nicene era came to be known as spiritual "fathers." Other designations for them are early fathers, church fathers, primitive fathers, and patristic fathers.

## WHY SHOULD WE LISTEN TO THEM TODAY?

Ante-Nicene fathers carried the torch of the Christian faith during and directly following the lifetimes of the apostles of Christ. One minor point on the definition of the word, "apostle" deserves explanation. Lately, church planters have sometimes been called apostles, and certainly, one of the spiritual gifts listed in Ephesians 4:11 is that of apostle. However, in the New Testament and in this book, the term "apostle" is associated with the men in Christ's inner circle of disciples or those specifically commissioned by Him, such as the apostle Paul. In the New Testament "the signs of a true apostle were performed ..

. by signs and wonders and miracles" (2 Corinthians 12:12).

Some of the earliest were actually taught by apostles. Irenaeus comments how his mentor Polycarp was instructed:

> Polycarp also was not only **instructed by apostles**, and conversed with many who had seen Christ, but was also, by apostles in Asia, appointed bishop of the church in Smyrna [St. John presiding per Tertullian], . . . and, when a very old man, gloriously and most nobly suffering martyrdom, departed this life, *having always taught the things which he had learned from the apostles,* and which the church has handed down.[2]

Another was Clement of Rome (not to be confused with Clement of Alexandria). According to tradition, Clement was a co-worker with the great apostle Paul and is believed to be the Clement that Paul refers to in Philippians 4:3: "Help these women who have shared my struggle in the cause of the gospel, together with Clement." But not only did Clement learn from Paul, he was also acquainted with other apostles, as Irenaeus remarks:

> In the third place from the apostles, Clement was allotted the bishopric [of Rome]. This man, as he had seen the blessed apostles, and had been **conversant with them**, might be said to have the preaching of the apostles still echoing [in his ears], and their traditions before his eyes. Nor was he alone [in this], for there were many still remaining who had received **instructions from the apostles**.[3]

Thus, early church history documents that some of the earliest Ante-Nicene fathers were taught the Holy Scriptures and doctrines of the Christian faith directly by apostles. In addition, apostles appointed some of the earliest Ante-Nicene fathers to church offices (episcopates), as Tertullian notes:

> This is the manner in which the apostolic churches transmit their registers: as the church of Smyrna, which records that Polycarp was placed therein by John [the apostle]; as also the church of Rome, which makes Clement to have been ordained in like manner by Peter [the apostle]. In exactly the same way the other churches ... [Ante-Nicene fathers] appointed to their episcopal places by apostles, they regard as transmitters of the apostolic seed [apostle's teachings].[4]

So, not only were the earliest Ante-Nicene fathers instructed in the Scriptures by apostles, some were appointed by them to their church leadership roles. Having been taught and appointed by apostles, older Ante-Nicene fathers in turn trained younger ministers some of whom also became known as Ante-Nicene fathers.

Yet, we should be careful to remember that unlike the divinely inspired Old Testament and New Testament books of the Bible, writings by the Ante-Nicene fathers were not inspired. Rather, their writings are comparable to books or other literature written by contemporary Christian leaders, who write about the Scriptures.

Still, what is unique about the Ante-Nicene fathers is the close proximity of their lives to the apostles of Christ. They were "witness to the authentically apostolic way of interpreting the Scriptures."[5] This is why we should listen to the Ante-Nicene fathers today, along with their perspectives on eschatology (theology of last things) to include their majority millennial view.

# 2

# THE FATHERS' MILLENNIAL VIEW

Proponents of every major prophecy interpretation (i.e. amillennialists, postmillennialists, preterists, and premillennialists or chiliasts) all cite writings by one or more Ante-Nicene father to support their millennial view. This should not come as a surprise, especially since unanimity on eschatology is rare in even one congregation, much less among multiple Ante-Nicene fathers on three continents who ministered over the course of almost three centuries.

Therefore, departure by some fathers from the Ante-Nicene fathers' majority millennial view would be expected. Among them were Caius of Rome and those associated with the School of Alexandria which emphasized the allegorical method of interpreting Scripture, e.g. Origen and his student Dionysius of Alexandria (aka the Great) who "went so far as to even deny that the apostle John wrote the book of Revelation."[1] Today, many fine and scholarly Christians hold a millennial view supported by these Ante-Nicene father's writings.

However, with regard to the majority millennial view of the Ante-Nicene church, Dr. Lewis Sperry Chafer, first president of Dallas Theological Seminary, writes: "Premillennialism was the all-but-universal belief of the early church;"[2] an interpretation of Scripture that Jesus Christ will return before (*pre*) the millennium.

Chafer's statement is affirmed by Dr. Philip Schaff (1819-1893), a leading expert on church history who served as dean of American church historians. Although Schaff was not a premillennialist (chiliast), but instead was a postmillennialist, he offered the following summary concerning the majority eschatological view of the Ante-Nicene age:

> The most striking point in the eschatology of the Ante-Nicene age is the prominent chiliasm [premillennialism], or millenarianism, that is the belief of a visible reign of Christ in glory on earth with the risen saints for a thousand years, before the general resurrection and [final] judgment. It was indeed not the doctrine of the church embodied in any creed or form of devotion, but a widely [held] current opinion of distinguished teachers.[3]

Here, church historian Schaff puts to rest the question as to what was the Ante-Nicene fathers' majority millennial view. He says that during the Ante-Nicene age chiliasm (premillennialism) was "a widely [held] current opinion of distinguished teachers," referring to the majority interpretation of Ante-Nicene fathers.

Who were these distinguished Ante-Nicene fathers who taught premillennialism? Following are brief biographies of just some Ante-Nicene premillennialists:

## PAPIAS (C. 70-155), BISHOP OF HIERAPOLIS

Papias wrote five books of which all but some fragments are lost. He reportedly conversed with "many who had known the Lord and His apostles. From these he gathered the floating traditions in regard to the sayings of our Lord, and wove them into a production divided into [his] five books."[4] According to Papias, "There will be a millennium after the resurrection from the dead, when the personal reign of Christ will be established on this earth."[5]

## JUSTIN MARTYR (C. 110–165)

The founder of theological literature, Justin Martyr was one of the great apologists of the early church, studied in the schools of the philosophers and was a disciple of Socrates and Plato. Justin noted, "There was a certain man with us, whose name was John, one of the apostles of Christ, who prophesied, by a revelation that was made to him, that those who believed in our Christ would dwell a thousand years [the millennium] in Jerusalem; and that thereafter the general, and, in short, the eternal resurrection and [final] judgment of all [spiritually lost] men would likewise take place."[6] Justin, a native of Palestine, also wrote about the relationship of Israel and the church. Under Roman Emperor Aurelius, Justin was martyred.

## IRENAEUS (C. 120–202), STUDENT OF POLYCARP

Irenaeus, Bishop of Lyons in France, is acclaimed as one of the greatest theologians of the second century. He grew up in Asia Minor under the tutelage of Polycarp, who had been taught by apostle John. Irenaeus authored a number of books, but he is best known for his five-volume *Against Heresies*. Irenaeus declared: "When this Antichrist shall have devastated all things in this world, he will reign for three years and six months, and sit in the temple at Jerusalem; and then the Lord will come from heaven in the clouds, in the glory of the Father . . . bringing in for the righteous the times of the kingdom [the millennium]."[7] Jerome, a church historian, wrote that Irenaeus was martyred.[8]

## HIPPOLYTUS (C. 170-236), STUDENT OF IRENAEUS

Bishop of Portus near Rome, Hippolytus is considered the most important theologian of the third century. Some of his greatest works were *On Christ and the Antichrist*, which survives complete; *Commentary on the Prophet Daniel*, and *The*

*Refutation of all Heresies,* in which he concludes the reason for "heresies, amid all their complexity and diversity . . . reduces to one common ground of censure — antagonism to Holy Scripture."[9] Hippolytus wrote, "The Sabbath is the type and emblem of the future kingdom [the millennium, or Sabbath-rest as it was called then] of the saints, when they 'shall reign with Christ,' when He comes from heaven."[10] Hippolytus joined the martyrs by being torn apart by wild horses.[11]

## Tertullian (c. 150–240), Founder of Latin Christianity

Presbyter of Carthage in North Africa, Tertullian "enjoyed a superior education, including literary, rhetorical, and legal training, as well as instruction in Greek and Latin."[12] As a young man he practiced law. About 185 Tertullian became a Christian and was appointed a presbyter c. 190. Although his native language was Greek, he was fluent in Latin and wrote Christian literature in this ancient Roman language becoming the founder of Latin Christianity. Tertullian, known for coining the term "Trinity" said, "We do confess that a kingdom is promised to us upon the earth . . . inasmuch as it will be after the resurrection for a thousand years."[13]

## Victorinus of Pettau (died c. 303/304), Theologian

Victorinus, Bishop of Pettau in Slovenia, authored commentaries on Genesis, Exodus, Leviticus, Isaiah, Ezekiel, Habakkuk, Ecclesiastes, Song of Solomon, Gospel of Matthew, and the Apocalypse (The Revelation). His only surviving works are his *Commentary on the Apocalypse of the Blessed John* and a short tract *On the Creation of the World.* Victorinus remarked, "Wherefore, as I have narrated, that true Sabbath [Sabbath-rest millennium] will be in the seventh millenary of years, when Christ with His elect shall reign."[14] During the persecutions of Roman Emperor Diocletian, Victorinus was martyred.

## LACTANTIUS (C. 250–325), LATIN SCHOLAR

Noted historian and apologist Lactantius grew up among the Roman elite. During the reign of Emperor Diocletian, he knew Constantine and considered him his friend. At the request of Diocletian, Lactantius became professor of rhetoric in Nicomedia (ancient city in Turkey), the favorite city of Diocletian. When Diocletian issued his first Edict of persecution against the Christians on February 24, 303, Lactantius lost his position as public teacher and was reduced to poverty. However, when his friend Constantine became emperor, Lactantius was elevated by him from penury to the palace, appointing him tutor in Latin to Constantine's son, Crispus. Lactantius authored a number of works, but he is best known for his great work, *The Divine Institutes,* in which he declares: "When the thousand years [the millennium] shall be completed, the world shall be renewed by God, and the heavens shall be folded together."[15]

Thus, it is established by early church writings and held by most of the scholarly community that the Ante-Nicene fathers' majority millennial view was premillennial. However, since a millennial interpretation is only one aspect of a broader eschatology, how does early church premillennialism compare to modern premillennial versions?

# 3

# PREMILLENNIAL VIEWS

Premillennialists today pitch their tents staunchly in two camps: historic premillennialism and pretribulational dispensational premillennialism. Of the two, the first represents an attempt at reclaiming the doctrine held by Ante-Nicene fathers, while the other diverged far from the writings of Irenaeus and his contemporaries.

Historic premillennialism (aka classic and covenantal premillennialism) was compiled by minority Protestant Reformers in the sixteenth century in their attempt to revive the premillennialism of the Ante-Nicene church. However, they were hindered in their efforts.

Obstacle number one was the conflict between Protestants and Catholics. Because of Reformation wars they were deterred from researching Ante-Nicene fathers' writings archived in Catholic churches.

Obstacle number two was Protestant tradition. The majority of Reformation Protestants retained amillennialism from their Catholic roots and were opposed to efforts to revive premillennialism. "The Augsburg Confession of 1530 by the Lutherans formally rejected premillennialism. Calvin regarded premillennialism as a 'fiction' that is 'too puerile to need or to deserve refutation.'"[1] And Michael Servetus (1511-1553), a Spanish theologian who taught premillennialism, was "condemned by Catholics and Protestants alike ... arrested in Geneva and burnt at the stake as a heretic."[2]

Therefore, meeting resistance in their efforts to research Ante-Nicene fathers writings, minority Reformers were unable to restore all features of early church premillennialism, as Chafer comments:

> Both justification by faith and chiliasm [premillennialism] are taught in the New Testament and were therefore the belief of the early church. These doctrines, like all other essential truths, went into obscurity during the Dark Ages. The Reformers did not restore all features of [early church premillennial] doctrine.[3]

Thus, even though historic premillennialism contains features of early church premillennialism, it does not mirror the premillennial teachings of the Ante-Nicene church.

The second iteration of premillennialism, pretribulational dispensational premillennialism (aka dispensationalism),was introduced in the nineteenth century by John Darby (1800-1881), then amended in the early twentieth century by Dr. C. I. Scofield (1843-1921).

Pretribulational dispensational premillennialism rapidly gained acceptance in the mid-twentieth century and is widely held today among conservative evangelicals. Yet, learned dispensationalists have conceded that dispensational premillennialism is not the premillennialism of the early church, a fact confirmed simply by reading Ante-Nicene premillennial writings.

The most refreshing aspect of early church premillennialism is that within its teachings the author finds not one contradiction in the Bible. This is the measure of accurately interpreting the sacred Word. Particularly significant are their teachings related to the relationship of Israel and the church.

# 4

# ISRAEL AND THE CHURCH

For twenty-eight years Germans in West Berlin and Germans in East Berlin were separated by a wall. In a historic speech in Berlin, U.S. President Reagan cried out to the President of the Soviet Union, "Mr. Gorbachev, tear down this wall!" Two years later the Berlin Wall toppled and the two groups became one people.

What about Israel and the church? Does a wall separate them? Are they two groups or one people?

Believers who divide all history into eras or dispensations hold that Israel and the church are two distinct groups, with two separate redemptive plans. Conversely, other Christians counter that the Bible teaches that spiritual Israel and the church are one people.

So, which is it?

Since you may be drawn into this debate you need to know biblical answers to the questions: What is the relationship of the church to Israel? When was the church founded? Is there an Israel within Israel? And, what answers do the Ante-Nicene fathers hold concerning these matters?

## WHAT IS THE RELATIONSHIP OF THE CHURCH TO ISRAEL?

Paul was a Hebrew of Hebrews, a highly educated Jewish leader and a zealous persecutor of Christians until he came to faith in Jesus Christ. Then, God's grace transformed him into the great apostle to the Gentiles and church planter. While imprisoned for his faith he wrote to the largely Gentile Ephesian church and explained to them the relationship the church to Israel:

> Remember that formerly you, the Gentiles in the flesh, who are called "Uncircumcision" by the so-called "Circumcision," which is performed in the flesh by human hands — remember that you were at that time separate from Christ, excluded from the commonwealth of Israel, and strangers to the covenants of promise, having no hope and without God in the world. But now in Christ Jesus you who formerly were far off have been brought near by the blood of Christ. For He Himself is our peace, who **made both groups into one** [spiritual Israel and the Gentile church] and broke down the barrier of the dividing wall, by abolishing in His flesh the enmity, which is the Law of commandments contained in ordinances, so that in Himself He might make the **two into one** new man, thus establishing peace, and might reconcile them both in one body to God through the cross, by it having put to death the enmity. And He came and preached peace to you who were far away, and peace to those who were near; for through Him we both have our access in one Spirit to the Father. So then you are no longer strangers and aliens, but you are fellow citizens with the saints, and are of God's household, having been built on the foundation of the apostles and [Old Testament] prophets, Christ Jesus Himself being the corner stone, in whom the whole building [the church, believing Jews and Gentiles], being fitted together, is growing into a holy temple in the Lord. (Ephesians 2:11-21)

Riddlebarger comments on this passage:

> Every major dispensational theologian ... insists that God has two distinct redemptive programs. ... Paul says that Jesus came to tear down the barrier wall which formerly divided

the two [Israel and the church], in order to make the two peoples into one so as to form Jew and Gentile together into the one living temple of the Lord—the church. . . . There is one people of God, the elect.[1]

Like the Berlin Wall that divided West and East Germans when it was broken down made both groups into one, Paul declares that the wall that divided Israel and the Gentile church when Jesus "broke" it down made "both groups into one" (Ephesians 2:14).

## WHEN WAS THE CHURCH FOUNDED?

Dispensationalists presume that Israel and the church are distinct because the church was not founded until Christ's advent. This supposition is based on Jesus telling His disciple, "You are Peter, and upon this rock I will build My church [Gk., *ekklesia*; assembly, congregation, or church]" (Matthew 16:18).

Yet, it should be remembered that before Christ came all mankind was in a state of sinfulness, because "all have sinned" (Romans 3:23). And because God requires sinlessness to enter heaven, this made salvation for mankind (Jew and Gentile) and the building of Christ's church impossible until His advent and atoning death for our sins.

Even though ancient Jews sacrificed animals, a foreshadowing of Christ's eventual once for all atoning sacrifice, realized salvation and the building of Christ's church was not possible until Christ's atoning sacrifice because "it is impossible for the blood of bulls and goats to take away sins" (Hebrews 10:4).

Only after Christ's atoning death on the cross was He able to "save His people from their sins" (Matthew 1:21); obtain redemption for all, Jew and Gentile; fulfill the prophecy of Genesis 3:15; and build His church with believing Jews and Gentiles.

### What about Old Testament Saints?

Before Christ's atoning sacrifice Old Testament saints at death were carried by angels to Paradise (Luke 23:43), also called "Abraham's bosom" (Luke 16:22), where they awaited the Savior's redemption that Christ would ultimately accomplish on the cross. While dying on the cross, Jesus spoke about Paradise to the thief who trusted in Him, saying, "Today you shall be with Me in Paradise" (Luke 23:43).

The Paradise about which Jesus spoke was not heaven where God the Father dwells. We know this because three days later at Christ's resurrection, Jesus told Mary Magdalene: "Stop clinging to Me, for I have **not** yet ascended to the Father" (John 20:17).

Forty days after Christ's resurrection, when Jesus was taken up into the clouds to heaven (Acts 1:4-11), Old Testament saints in Paradise accompanied Him for "when He ascended on high, He led captive a host of captives" (Ephesians 4:8).

Thus, after Christ's atoning sacrifice "for sins once for all, the just for the unjust, so that He might bring us to God" (1 Peter 3:18), Jesus was then able to build His church by putting the pieces together so-to-speak—Old Testament Jewish and Gentile saints added to growing numbers of New Testament saints—forming the body of Christ, the church, that "is growing into a holy temple in the Lord" (Ephesians 2:21). This was foreshadowed in the Old Testament.

## Old Testament Foreshadowing of the Temple

In Scripture "the son of David" (2 Chronicles 1:1) refers to the son of ancient Israel's King David, namely, King Solomon. But elsewhere in Scripture the phrase refers to David's descendant, "the Son of David," Jesus Christ (Matthew 10:47).

King Solomon is credited with building the first temple. Yet long **before** Solomon began to build, while he was still a lad, his father David was making preparations for the temple. "David . . . set stone-cutters to hew out stones to build the house of God. And David prepared . . . cedar logs beyond number. . . . So David made ample preparations before his death" (1 Chronicles 22:2-5). In his latter days David told his son: "I have prepared for the house of the LORD [the temple] 100,000 talents of gold . . . also timber and stone I have prepared, and you may **add to them**" (1 Chronicles 22:14).

Just as Solomon, the son of David, built the physical temple with materials beyond number that his father helped prepare and **added to them**, so Jesus Christ, the Son of David, is building the holy temple, the church, with saints beyond number that His Father helped prepare in Old Testament times and Christ is **adding to them** (believing Jews and Gentiles) in New Testament times.

Therefore, what was foreshadowed in the Old Testament with the building of the physical temple was fulfilled in the New Testament with the building of the holy temple, the church: "Christ Jesus Himself being the corner stone, in whom the whole building, being fitted together, is growing into a holy temple in the Lord" (Ephesians 2:20,21).

## IS THERE AN ISRAEL WITHIN ISRAEL?

Certainly, from a human perspective all Israelites are part of Israel. But not from God's perspective, since His Word says: "They are **not** all Israel who are descended from Israel" (Romans 9:6). God views Israel as two kingdoms: "**spiritual Israel**," a saved remnant that is also called the "true Israel" and "the Israel of God" (Galatians 6:16); and "**national Israel**," that is also called "unbelieving Israel." These two kingdoms were foreshadowed in the Old Testament.

The smaller southern kingdom, typifying spiritual Israel, numbered only two tribes, Judah and Benjamin, who worshipped Holy God at the temple in Jerusalem. In stark contrast, the larger northern kingdom representing unbelieving national Israel numbered ten tribes who worshipped idols of golden calves at Bethel (1 Kings 12:25-33). These two kingdoms, the Israel within Israel, are illustrated by Paul through the divine response to the prophet Elijah:

> Do you not know what the Scripture says in the passage about Elijah, how he pleads with God against Israel [unbelieving national Israel]? "Lord, they have killed your prophets, they have torn down your altars, and I alone am left, and they are seeking my life." But what is the divine

response to him? "I have kept for Myself seven thousand men [spiritual Israel] who have not bowed the knee to Baal." In the same way then, there has also come to be at the present time a remnant according to God's gracious choice. (Romans 11:2-5)

Here, Paul makes a clear distinction between the saved remnant, "spiritual Israel," and the larger unbelieving "national Israel." The *New Bible Commentary* adds:

Paul suggests, in keeping with the Old Testament 'remnant' theology, a spiritual Israel within a larger ethnic Israel. . . . Paul proves his point about the Israel within Israel in two roughly parallel arguments drawn from Old Testament history.[2]

Paul also confirms by citing the divine response to Elijah that spiritual Israel who was present in Old Testament times "has also come to be at the present time [in New Testament times]" (Romans 11:5). Therefore, the Bible clearly affirms the continuation of the Old Testament people of God, spiritual Israel, in New Testament times.

Further, Paul confirms in this epistle who it is from Israel that will be saved:

Though the number of the sons of Israel be as the sand of the sea, it is the remnant [spiritual Israel] that will be saved. (Romans 9:27)

From this verse it is evident that those identified with the larger ethnic Israel, unbelieving national Israel, who "built the high places of Baal that are in the valley of Ben-hinnom to cause their sons and their daughters to pass through the fire to Molech, which I [God] had not commanded them" (Jeremiah 32:35); who "kills the prophets and stones those who are sent to her!" (Matthew 23:37); and who "crucified the Lord of glory" (1 Corinthians 2:8), will not be saved.

## National Israel's Disobedience and Disbelief

Because of national Israel's disobedience and disbelief in Jesus as their Messiah, Jesus foretold with a parable that the kingdom of God would be taken away from them and given to the Gentiles:

> There was a landowner who planted a vineyard . . . and rented it out to vine-growers and went on a journey. When the harvest time approached, he sent his slaves to the vine-growers to receive his produce. The vine-growers took his slaves and beat one, and killed another [analogous to Old Testament prophets martyred], and stoned a third. . . . Afterward he sent his son [analogous to Jesus], . . . [but] they took him, and threw him out of the vineyard and killed him. . . . Jesus said to them, "Did you never read in the Scriptures, 'The stone which the builders rejected, this became the chief corner stone; . . . Therefore I say to you, the kingdom of God will be taken away from you [unbelieving national Israel] and given to a people [Gentiles], producing the fruit of it. (Matthew 21:33-43)

The Gentile church that would come to faith in Jesus Christ was foretold in the Old Testament: "A people [Gentiles] whom I did not know became subject to Me: They were obedient to the hearing of My ear" (2 Samuel 22:44-45). And, "I was found of them [Gentiles] who sought Me not; I became manifest to those who inquired not after Me" (Isaiah 65:1).

Because of national Israel's disobedience and rejection of Jesus Christ, even crucifying the Lord of glory, those and other Old Testament prophesies about the Gentile church were fulfilled. As the Bible says: "By their [national Israel's] transgression salvation has come to the Gentiles" (Romans 11:11).

## Salvation Comes to the Gentiles

Acts Chapter 10 is the first New Testament account of salvation coming to the Gentiles. It came as a surprise to the early Israelite church (spiritual Israel) that Gentiles could come to saving faith in

Jesus Christ and become a part of the people of God, Israel.

## Gentile Church Grafted into Israel

Paul uses the analogy of a figurative olive tree and a figurative wild olive branch to explain how the Gentile church was grafted into Israel:

> But if some of the branches [national Israel] were broken off, and you, being a wild olive [Gentile church], were **grafted in among them** [spiritual Israel] and became partaker with them of the rich root of the olive tree [Israel], do not be arrogant toward the branches; but if you are arrogant, remember that it is not you who supports the root, but the root [patriarchs of Israel] supports you. You will say then, "Branches were broken off so that I [Gentile church] might be grafted in." Quite right, they were broken off for their unbelief, but you stand by your faith. . . . And they also, if they [national Israel] do not continue in their unbelief, will be grafted in, for God is able to graft them in again. For if you [Gentile church] were cut off from what is by nature a wild olive tree, and were grafted contrary to nature into a cultivated olive tree [Israel], how much more will these who are the natural branches [national Israel] be grafted into their own olive tree? For I do not want you, brethren, to be uninformed of this mystery – so that you will not be wise in your own estimation – that a partial hardening has happened to Israel until the fullness of the Gentiles has come in; and so all Israel will be saved. (Romans 11:17-26)

With this analogy to the horticultural technique of grafting, the apostle Paul portrays the Gentile church being grafted into Israel, Jesus having "made both groups into one" (Ephesians 2:14). Having been grafted into Israel, Carson reminds the Gentile church not to forget our Jewish heritage:

> They [the Gentile church] are not to forget that the root of the olive tree into which they have been grafted is itself

Jewish, for God's people are built on his promises to, and dealings with, the patriarchs (*cf.* also [Rom.] 4:11–12, 16–17; Gal. 3:15–29). The church to which the Gentile Christians in Rome belong is nothing less than the continuation of the one people of God from the Old Testament [spiritual Israel].[3]

## All Israel Will Be Saved

The modern-day State of Israel is a continuation of national Israel within which there is a remnant of believing Jews, spiritual Israel, the church. National Israel as an ethnic group rejects Jesus as their Messiah.

Although many evangelical Christians, including the author, respect the modern-day State of Israel, the truth is if Jesus Christ came to Israel today He would be treated just as cruelly by them as He was nearly two thousand years ago. This, a National Prayer Network special report *Christians in Israel: An Endangered Species* affirms: "A spirit of anti-Christ persecution pervades the "Holy Land." Little has changed in 2,000 years.'"[4]

Nevertheless, even though contemporary national Israel, as with ancient Israel, is in a state of unbelief, apostle Paul foresaw contemporary national Israel coming to saving faith in Jesus Christ after "the fullness of the Gentiles has come in" (Romans 11:25). Consequently, when today's national Israel comes to repentance and saving faith in Jesus as their Messiah and Lord, they will be grafted back "into their own olive tree" (Romans 11:24) joining their brethren spiritual Israel and the grafted in Gentile church who already comprise the olive tree, Israel (Romans 11:17).

Then "all Israel will be saved" (Romans 11:26); that is, all spiritual Israel which includes Old Testament and New Testament spiritual Israel, converted contemporary national Israel, and grafted in Gentile believers. This whole company of regenerate persons (Jew and Gentile) is variously called in Scripture as "the Israel of God" (Galatians 6:16); the "holy temple in the Lord" (Ephesians 2:21); "the elect" (2 Timothy 2:10); "the bride, the wife of the Lamb" (Revelation 21:9); "the body of Christ" (1 Corinthians 12:27); and "the household of God, which is the church" (1 Timothy 3:15).

A.H. Strong, nineteenth century scholar and author of *Systematic Theology* comments: "The church of Christ, in its largest signification, is the whole company of regenerate persons [believing Jews and Gentiles] in all times and ages, in heaven and on earth (Mat. 16:18; Eph. 1:22, 23; 3:10; 5:24, 5:25; Col. 1:18; Heb. 12:23)."[5]

## The Fathers' Teachings on Israel and the Church

Ignatius, who studied under the apostle John and who served as Bishop of Antioch, "did view the church as the continuation of the Old Testament people of God [spiritual Israel.]"[6]

Justin Martyr comments likewise:

> The true spiritual Israel, and descendants of Judah, Jacob, Isaac, and Abraham (who in uncircumcision was approved of and blessed by God on account of his faith, and called the father of many nations), are **we** [the church, Jew and Gentile] who have been led to God through this crucified Christ.[7]

Tertullian declares that when Christ returns that Gentile believers will be gathered in with the saved remnant of Israel:

> For after He [Jesus] had declared that 'Jerusalem was to be trodden down of the Gentiles, until the times of the Gentiles should be fulfilled' [Luke 21:24],— meaning, of course, those which were to be chosen of God, and gathered in with the remnant of Israel [spiritual Israel].[8]

Tertullian also remarks in reference to Hosea 1:10 and 1 Peter 2:10:

> We [believing Gentiles], who "were not the people of God" in days bygone, have been made His people [spiritual Israel].[9]

So, are Israel and the church two groups or one people? The Holy Scriptures and the early church Ante-Nicene fathers teachings are crystal clear about the relationship of Israel and the church that Jesus Christ has "made both groups into one" (Ephesians 2:14).

Now that we have a biblical understanding of the relationship of the churchto Israel, we can gain a biblical understanding of prophecy. And a key to understanding Bible prophecy is the foretold "seventy weeks" of Daniel.

# 5

# THE SEVENTIETH WEEK

During World War II thousands of allied troops waited in full knowledge that the D-Day invasion was coming. What they didn't know was the date the invasion would begin.

Today, many believers know from Scripture that the prophesied seventieth week is coming. What we don't know is the date it will begin. However, the Old Testament prophet, Daniel, foretold what will signal the beginning of the seventieth week and what the seventy weeks will entail. He describes it in the famous seventy weeks prophecy:

> Seventy weeks have been decreed for your people and your holy city, to finish the transgression, to make an end of sin, to make atonement for iniquity, to bring in everlasting righteousness, to seal up vision and prophecy and to anoint the most holy place. So you are to know and discern that from the issuing of a decree to restore and rebuild Jerusalem until Messiah the Prince there will be seven weeks and sixty-two weeks; it will be built again, with plaza and moat, even in times of distress. Then after the sixty-two weeks the Messiah will be cut off and have nothing, and the people of the prince who is to come will destroy the city and the sanctuary. And

its end will come with a flood; even to the end there will be war; desolations are determined. And he will make a firm covenant with the many for **one week** [the seventieth week], but in the middle of the week he will put a stop to sacrifice and grain offering; and on the wing of abominations will come one who makes desolate, even until a complete destruction, one that is decreed, is poured out on the one who makes desolate. (Daniel 9:24-27)

According to this prophecy, at the end of seventy weeks sin will "end" and "everlasting righteousness" will begin. In other words, when the seventy weeks conclude, life as we know it will dramatically change.

This begs the questions: What is the duration of the seventy weeks? What are the major interpretations of the seventy weeks? Is seventy weeks a divine time measurement? Will the Gentile church be affected when the seventieth week begins? And, what signals the start of the seventieth week?

## What Is the Duration of the Seventy Weeks?

It was disclosed to Daniel that seventy weeks, or literally a period of seventy sevens, "have been decreed for your people [Israel] and your holy city [Jerusalem]" (v. 24). In ancient Israel, Jews thought in seven-year units (heptads), so the seventy weeks are generally held to be "sevens" of years. This is proven by calculating the year of Jubilee that occurred every fiftieth year. To calculate it, the Lord instructed ancient Jews to "count off seven sabbaths of years — seven times seven years — so that the seven sabbaths of years amount to a period of forty-nine years," (Leviticus 25:8 NIV) bringing them to the year of Jubilee.

Therefore, since a sabbath of years is a period of seven years, a prophetic week is held to be a period of seven years. Ante-Nicene father Hippolytus also interpreted a prophetic week to be seven years, saying that by "one week, he indicated seven years."[1] Therefore, it is generally held that the duration of the prophesied seventy weeks is 490 years (70 weeks x 7 years each).

## MAJOR INTERPRETATIONS OF THE SEVENTY WEEKS?

Although there are variations, scholars hold four major interpretations about the seventy weeks, or 490 years:

> **Literal Years Beginning 586 BC:** They are literal years that extend from Jerusalem's fall in 586 BC to the end of persecutions by Antiochus IV Epiphanes (either when the temple was cleansed in 164 BC or at Antiochus's death in 163 BC). The problems with this view are: One, Daniel's prophecy specifically states that the seventy weeks begin "from the issuing of a decree to restore and rebuild Jerusalem" (v. 25), and there is no known decree to rebuild Jerusalem at the time of its fall in 586 BC. Two, the duration is shorter than 490 years (seventy weeks) by about 67 years.

> **Symbolic Periods from 538 BC forward:** The seventy weeks are symbolic periods of time that extend from Cyrus's decree in about 538 BC that allowed the Jewish exiles to return to their homeland to the first century, but before the fall of Jerusalem in AD 70, covering a span of about 607 years. The problems with this view are similar to the first. One, Cyrus did not issue a decree to restore and rebuild Jerusalem, only to rebuild the temple (2 Chronicles 36:23). Two, the duration exceeds 490 years (seventy weeks) by about 117 years.

> **Symbolic of Church History Timeframes:** The seventy weeks are symbolic periods that prophesy about church history (Old Testament and New Testament) and extend from Cyrus's decree in 538 BC to the end of days when Christ returns to earth. This view does not interpret literally the rebuilding of Jerusalem. The problems with this view are: One, its figurative interpretations are highly subjective. Two, the elapsed time from Cyrus's decree to Christ's return to

earth at the end of days exceeds 490 years, or seventy weeks, by several centuries.

➢ **Literal Years Beginning 445 BC:** These are literal years that begin with the decree of the Persian King Artaxerxes Longimanus in the twentieth year of his reign on the generally held date of 445 BC (Nehemiah 2:1-8) that granted permission to the Jews to rebuild Jerusalem's city walls. Daniel was told that "the issuing of a decree to restore and rebuild Jerusalem" (v. 25) would start the seventy weeks.

Ante-Nicene father Julius Africanus also held that the seventy weeks began with Artaxerxes decree, saying:

The seventy weeks which make up 490 years the angel instructs us to take from the going forth of the commandment to answer and to build Jerusalem. And this happened in the twentieth year of the reign of Artaxerxes, King of Persia. For Nehemiah his cup-bearer besought him, and received the answer that Jerusalem should be built.[2]

A note regarding the fourth interpretation. It also holds that the seventy weeks will have three segments: seven weeks, sixty-two weeks, and one week.

➢ **Seven Weeks:** The first segment of "seven weeks" (49 years) are for the rebuilding of Jerusalem as foretold to Daniel who said, "From the issuing of a decree to restore and rebuild Jerusalem ... there will be **seven weeks** ... it will be built again, with plaza and moat, even in times of distress" (v. 25).

➢ **Sixty-Two Weeks:** After completion of the seven weeks (49 years) there will be a segment of "sixty-two weeks" (434 years) for a combined total of sixty-nine weeks (7 + 62), or 483 years, that extend to the first coming of the Messiah,

Jesus Christ, foretelling when He would be put to death. As Daniel foretold, "Then after the **sixty-two weeks** the Messiah will be cut off (Heb., *karat*, cut off, cut down, or put to death)" (v. 26). Here, there is a gap.

➢ **One Week** (the seventieth week): After the sixty-ninth week ends, the seventy weeks prophecy does not resume until the time of "the prince who is to come" (v. 26), namely, the Antichrist. At that time, "he [the Antichrist] will make a firm covenant with the many for one week [the seventieth week]" (v. 27), at the conclusion of which the seventy weeks, or 490 years, will be complete.

The "Literal Years Beginning 445 BC" interpretation is widely held among conservative evangelicals, but it has one problem. The decree of Artaxerxes that granted permission to the Jews to rebuild Jerusalem on the generally held date of 445 BC until Christ's crucifixion after the 69th week, or after 483 years, falls short and does not add up to 483 years. There have been various attempts to explain this inconsistency, all of which seem lacking, except when recognizing the following two points:

**Gregorian Calendar Error**: The Gregorian calendar dates from the birth of Christ. Though it is believed that Jesus was 33 ½ years old when He was crucified, the Gregorian calendar has been found to be in error by four to six years due to a miscalculation in the sixth century, as King Herod who attempted to kill Jesus as a baby died in 4 BC. Consequently, the estimated time of Christ's crucifixion is about AD 28-30.

**Decree of Artaxerxes**: Calculating this as the start of the seventy weeks in the year of 445 BC to Christ's crucifixion after the 69th week in about AD 28 totals to only **473 years** (445 + 28 = 473), not **483 years**. Thus, an earlier date of about 455 BC for the start of the seventy weeks would be needed to equate to 483 years. Aware of this inconsistency, some scholars have attempted to date the seventy weeks from the Old Testament prophet Ezra. But there is no mention in

Scripture that Ezra had the king's permission to rebuild Jerusalem, and the earlier Ezra date results in too many years until Christ's crucifixion at the end of the 69th week. Others have attempted to arrive at the 483 years by using an assumed 360-day lunar year, but the lunar year is 354.37 days with intercalary adjustments that were used by the Jews and the Greeks to equate the lunar calendar with the solar calendar. So, lunar computations do not yield the expected result.

Consequently, the question is: How accurate is the presumed date of 445 BC for the twentieth year of Artaxerxes? Remarking about this are Keil and Delitzsch in the *Commentary on the Old Testament*:

> We will not urge against the precise accuracy of the fulfillment arrived at by this calculation, that the *terminus a quo* adopted by Hengstenberg, viz., the twentieth year of Artaxerxes, coincides with the 455th year B.C. only on the supposition that Xerxes reigned but eleven years, and that Artaxerxes came to the throne ten years earlier than the common reckoning, according to which Xerxes reigned twenty-one years, and that the correctness of this view is opposed by Hofm., Kleinert, Wieseler, and others, because the arguments for and against it are evenly balanced; but with Preiswerk, whose words Auderlen quotes with approbation, considering **the uncertainty of ancient chronology on many points**, we shall not lay stress on calculating the exact year, but shall regard the approximate coincidence of the prophetical with the historical time as a sufficient proof that there may be possibly have been an exact correspondence in the number of years, and that no one, at all events, can prove the contrary.[3]

Accordingly, as Keil and Delitzsch assert, because of "the uncertainty of ancient chronology on many points" (e.g. the Gregorian calendar is in error by four to six years) "the approximate coincidence of the prophetical with the historical time" is sufficient proof that from the decree of Artaxerxes in the twentieth year of his reign until the Messiah, Jesus Christ, who was slain for the sin of the world after the sixty-ninth week, or in about AD 28-30, equates to 483 years "and that no one, at all events, can prove the contrary."

Therefore, it is held that only one week remains for Israel, the seventieth, of the seventy weeks.

## IS SEVENTY WEEKS A DIVINE TIME MEASUREMENT?

Timelines of the Bible are available in Christian bookstores and online. Or you can save some money and calculate for yourself the record of biblical time by counting the ages of fathers at children's birth, the duration of king's reigns, etc. As you document the timeline, you may notice a pattern. Significant events occur at seventy week intervals, which begs the question: Is seventy weeks a divine time measurement? The timeline of Israel may hold a clue.

### Israel's Timeline

National Israel began when God changed Jacob's name to Israel (Genesis 32:28). How old was Jacob when this happened? The Bible does not state it directly, but does provide the following sequence of events to approximate his age:

➢ Jacob (Israel) was **130** years old when he moved to Egypt (Genesis 47:9).

➢ Jacob's son Joseph was age 30 when he was presented before Pharaoh (Genesis 41:46). Afterwards, there were seven years of plenty and two years of famine (Genesis 45:6), or nine years elapsed, making Joseph at least age 39 when his father Jacob at age 130 came to Egypt. Subtracting, this made Jacob at Joseph's birth about **ninety** (if months are accounted for) or ninety-one.

➢ According to Genesis 30:25, after Joseph was born Jacob told his father-in-law Laban to "send me away, that I may go to my own place and to my own country." With a new baby his departure was probably not immediate. During Jacob's trip back home God changed Jacob's name to Israel (Genesis 32:28) when Jacob was likely **age 90**.

Thus, the timeline for Israel: National Israel began when the patriarch Israel was likely age 90. About forty years later, Israel (Jacob at age 130) moved with his family to Egypt. After that the history of Israel contains four seventy-week periods (4 x 490 years each) which can be added from the biblical record for a total dispensation of about 2,000 years (40 years + (4 x 490 years each) of which all but seven years have been completed.

Therefore, Israel has likely fulfilled 1,993 years of her probable 2,000 year dispensation. *The New American Commentary* calculates a similar timeline for national Israel: "God focused his attention on the Jewish people for about two thousand years."[4]

## Ancient Gentiles Timeline

Interestingly, when you compute biblical time backwards from the beginning of national Israel (when God changed Jacob's name to Israel) to Adam, indications are that the ancient Gentiles (e.g. Enoch, Noah) may have also had a timeline like national Israel—an initial forty year period plus four seventy-week prophetic periods—that go back to what may have been the Fall beginning this present evil age.

However, we cannot be certain because the Scriptures do not state the age of Adam when he fell into sin. Yet, the Bible reveals that Adam was 130 years old when his son, Seth, was born while he and Eve were living outside the garden **after** the Fall (Genesis 5:3). Interestingly, when the same timeline as Israel's (40 years + (4 x 490 years each), or 2,000 years, is applied to the ancient Gentiles it extends well before Adam's 130th year allowing ample time for their first son Cain to be born and to grow to an age and stature sufficient for him to tend crops and to murder his younger brother Abel (Genesis 4:8).

Of note, some Bible chronologists become frustrated when their documentation of biblical time does not match secular dating. Be reminded of the scholars Keil and Delitzsch remark about "the uncertainty of ancient chronology on many points."[5]

What about the timeline of the modern-day Gentiles?

## Modern-Day Gentiles Timeline

Sandwiched between the end of Israel's sixty-ninth week (Daniel 9:26) and the resumption of Israel's seventieth week (Daniel 9:27) is "the times of the [modern-day] Gentiles" (Luke 21:24). Jesus foretold about the modern-day Gentile dispensation saying that the Jews "will fall by the edge of the sword, and will be led captive into all the nations; and Jerusalem will be trampled underfoot by the Gentiles **until the times of the Gentiles are fulfilled**" (Luke 21:24).

The modern-day Gentile dispensation (perhaps like Israel's and the ancient Gentiles) may have also started with an initial forty year period. About forty years after religious Jews instigated the unjust crucifixion of the Messiah, Jesus Christ (a type of Passover Lamb of God), judgment fell on the Jewish people. In the mid AD 60's Judean Jews rebelled against their Roman masters, but "by the year 68 resistance in the northern part of the province had been eradicated and the Romans turned their full attention to the subjugation of Jerusalem."[6] Two years later on 14 April 70, during Passover, the Roman General Titus and his legions laid siege to Jerusalem subsequently destroying the city and the temple.

Thus, the elapsed time from the end of Israel's sixty-ninth week (after which the Messiah, Jesus Christ, was "cut off," or crucified, in about AD 28-30) to the Roman campaign to subjugate Jerusalem in AD 68 or to the Fall of Jerusalem in AD 70 was likely **forty years**.

Since then, three seventy-week periods have been completed with a fourth nearing completion. All total, since AD 28-30 almost 2,000 years (40 years + (4 x 490 years each) have elapsed for the modern-day Gentiles.

How many seventy-week periods will God allow for the modern-day Gentile dispensation? Only God knows. However, Jesus did reveal when the modern-day Gentile dispensation will end saying, "Jerusalem will be trampled underfoot by the Gentiles until the times of the Gentiles are fulfilled" (Luke 21:24).

In other words, when the Israeli-Palestinian peace process or a conflict in the region enables Israel to gain full control of Jerusalem and its ancient temple site, this will be an indication that the modern-day Gentile dispensation is about to end and that Israel's seventieth week is about to begin.

## THE GENTILE CHURCH AND THE SEVENTIETH WEEK

Millions of Christians today believe that the church will be raptured before the start of the seventieth week. However, this belief is just the opposite of what the Bible teaches, **because:**

Israel (both national and spiritual Israel) has one week, or seven years, to fulfill in order to complete Israel's allotted dispensation. According to Romans 11:17 the Gentile church was grafted into spiritual Israel "and became partaker with them of the rich root of the olive tree [Israel]," Christ Jesus having "made both groups into **one**" (Ephesians 2:14). Therefore, since spiritual Israel must absolutely be on the earth during Israel's seventieth week so they can complete Israel's dispensation, this means that the Gentile church that was grafted into spiritual Israel (Romans 11:17) must also absolutely be on the earth during the seventieth week, the final seven years, or the equivalent time thereof. (See equivalent time explanation).

**Equivalent Time**: Must spiritual Israel, the church, be on the earth the entire final seven years? No! Why not? Because in the Bible numbers are routinely rounded. A case in point was the chronology of construction of Solomon's Temple:

> Solomon began to build the house of the Lord in Jerusalem. . . . He began to build on the second day in the **second month** of the **fourth year** of his reign. (2 Chronicles 3:1-2)

> In the fourth year the foundation of the house of the Lord was laid, in the month of Ziv [second month in Judean calendar]. In the **eleventh year**, in the month of Bul, which is the **eighth month**, the house was finished throughout all its parts and according to all its plans. So he was **seven years** in building it. (1 Kings 6:37-38)

Let's calculate. Solomon began construction of the temple in the **fourth year, second month,** and second day of his reign. He completed the temple in the **eleventh year, eighth month** of his reign, or in slightly less than **seven years, six months**. Yet, the Bible records

44

the duration: "He was **seven years** in building it" (1 Kings 6:38).

Therefore, because of rounding in Scripture, six years and seven months is equivalent to seven years, biblically speaking. This is why the church, spiritual Israel, will not need to be on the earth the entire final seven years, the seventieth week.

Thus, the church, spiritual Israel, can be raptured before the start of the wrath of the Lamb judgments of The Revelation that will occur in the final months of the seventieth week (see Revelation 9:5,10). Early church premillennialists taught that the church will be raptured before the wrath of the Lamb judgments begin. (More on this later).

## WHAT SIGNALS THE START OF THE SEVENTIETH WEEK?

A ceremonious signing of a covenant will start the seventieth week, as Daniel foretold:

> The **prince** [the Antichrist] who is to come . . . he will make a firm covenant with the many for one week [the seventieth week]. (Daniel 9:27)

When Daniel first mentions this "prince who is to come" he related — **not** about him — but about his people who would "destroy the city" Jerusalem in AD 70. Therefore, the prince did not come then (in AD 70), but his people did. As Daniel said, "The **people** of the prince who is to come will destroy the city [Jerusalem] and the sanctuary [the temple]" (v. 26).

Who were those people who came in AD 70 and destroyed Jerusalem? Romans! Who are the people of the prince who is to come? The people of a restored Roman Empire. From this European Union (the name may change when it federalizes) will come the **prince** (the Antichrist).

As the future ruler of this restored Roman Empire, the Antichrist will make a covenant with "the many" (v. 27). Interpretations vary as to who "the many" are, but the angelic messenger seems to make it clear when he tells Daniel that this prophecy is "for your people [Israel]" (v. 24).

Therefore, as president or emperor of the restored Roman Empire, the Antichrist on behalf of his government will make a covenant with "the many" people of Israel for "one week" (i.e. seven years). Presumably, this covenant will promise protection and religious liberty to the Jews, permitting them to perform animal sacrifices and grain offerings in their future rebuilt Jerusalem temple in exchange for some favor, perhaps their worship of him. The Bible says, "All who dwell on the earth will worship him, whose names have not been written in the Book of Life of the Lamb" (Revelation 13:8 NKJV).

Many Jewish people who are anti-Christian like their forefathers will initially esteem the Antichrist as their long-awaited messiah. About this, Ante-Nicene father Irenaeus quotes Jesus in John 5:43 regarding how the Jews rejected Him as their Messiah but will accept the Antichrist as their messiah:

> "I have come in my Father's name, and ye have not received Me: when another shall come in his own name, him ye will receive," calling Antichrist "the other."[7]

This was foreshadowed at the trial of Jesus. Pilate the governor was attempting to free Jesus because he told the Jews, "I find no guilt in Him" (John 18:38). But knowing that the Jews had a custom that the governor would release at the Passover one prisoner, Pilate brought out a notorious criminal named Barabbas, a murderer and a robber, and asked the Jews: "Whom do you want me to release for you? Barabbas, or Jesus who is called Christ?" (Matthew 27:17). The Jews chose Barabbas, a murderer and a robber [a type of the Antichrist], but for Jesus they cried out, "Crucify Him!" (Matthew 27:22).

Like their forefathers, national Israel will initially esteem a murderer and a robber, the Antichrist, as their long-awaited messiah. However, the smooth-tongued Antichrist will soon break his covenant with Israel. As Daniel says, "In the middle of the week he will put a stop to sacrifice and grain offering" (v. 27), breaking his covenant. About this covenant-breaker the Psalmist prophesies:

He has put forth his hands against those who were at peace with him [Israel]; he has violated his covenant. His speech was smoother than butter, but his heart was war. (Psalm 55:20-21)

So, is the seventieth week about to begin?

A similar question was on the minds of allied troops in England in April and May 1944 who asked—is the D-Day invasion about to begin? The date was not revealed to them, of course. But they could observe thousands of troops arriving and a massive buildup of armaments and recognize that the date for the start of D-Day may not be far away.

Similarly, only God knows the date when the seventieth week will begin. But we can observe that after centuries of diaspora the Jews have returned to their homeland. Further, the modern State of Israel continues to thrive and be in a position to fulfill their end time prophecies. Thus, we should acknowledge that the start of the seventieth week may not be far away.

When it does begin, the tribulation will be close at hand. This is a subject that early church premillennialists, and the church-at-large for almost nineteen centuries, interpreted differently from what is popularly taught today. So we can't help but wonder if the tribulation is misunderstood today?

# 6

# TIME, TIMES AND HALF A TIME

In its original sense "tribulation" means "grinding corn." The Romans ground corn and other grains with a *tribulum*. It was a heavy wooden sledge composed of two flat timbered planks (top and bottom). Underneath the top plank were attached metal spikes or stones. When the top plank was raised, it allowed corn or wheat to be placed between the planks. When the heavy top plank was released upon (or rolled over) the bottom plank, it crushed and ground the corn or wheat into corn meal or flour.

This practice of grinding corn or crushing wheat with a *tribulum* became analogous to early Christians of their sufferings from persecution. Persecuted Roman Christians felt like they were being crushed and ground by a *tribulum*. And so, from the Latin *tribulum* was derived the English word "tribulation."

In Scripture the Greek word *thlípsis* means to crush or to press together and is variously translated as tribulation, persecution, distress, suffering, hardship, trouble, anguish, and affliction. Throughout church history believers in Jesus Christ have suffered tribulation (persecution). Most Christians acknowledge this as *The Complete Word Study Dictionary* explains:

> Christians are not exempt from tribulation, but rather they are especially subject to it. Their tribulation consists largely of persecution and the opposition their testimony meets in an unfriendly world. "The persecution that arose

about Stephen" (Acts 11:19), was, of course, *thlipsis*. Paul speaks of all the "persecutions and tribulations" which the Thessalonians endured (2 Thess. 1:4). They received the word "with much tribulation" . . . and Paul entreats them not to "be moved by these tribulations." . . . In 2 Cor. 8:2, we are told that the churches of Macedonia experienced much tribulation.[1]

Jesus foretold that just prior to His return there will be a period of tribulation. Historically, Christians interpreted Scripture to teach that the end of days tribulation will be a time of persecution that will befall the church at the hands of the Antichrist. Ante-Nicene father and bishop Hippolytus affirmed: "Now, concerning **the tribulation of the persecution which is to fall upon the church** from the adversary [the Antichrist]."[2]

However, in the early twentieth century this understanding changed when a leading dispensationalist reinterpreted the end of days tribulation both in duration and substance. As a result, this chapter will address the duration of the tribulation, the substance of the tribulation, and Ante-Nicene fathers' teachings about the tribulation, and why the Tribulation is misunderstood today.

## DURATION OF THE TRIBULATION

For most of the first nineteen centuries of the Christian faith the majority of church scholars interpreted the Bible to teach that the end of days tribulation period (tribulation and great tribulation) will have a total duration of "a time, times, and half a time" (Daniel 12:7). A "time" being one year, "times" being two years, and "half a time" being half a year, or about three and one-half years (rounded) within the final seven years, the seventieth week.

Even John Darby (1800-1881), the nineteenth century founder of dispensationalism and pretribulational dispensational premillennialism, held that the duration of the tribulation period (tribulation and great tribulation) will be as stated in the Bible for "a time, times, and half a time" (Daniel 12:7). However, after the passing of Darby, other dispensationalists gained prominence, one of whom was Dr. C. I. Scofield (1843-1921). In the early twentieth century Scofield introduced a theory that reinterpreted the duration of the end of days tribulation.

## Scofield's Influence

Dr. Scofield theorized that the tribulation period encompasses not just a "time, times, and half a time" (Daniel 12:7), or about three and one-half years within the seventieth week, but **all** seven of the final seven years. In his work *Prophecy Made Plain* Scofield explains how he arrived at a seven-year tribulation interpretation. He begins by replying to his own question:

> What will be the Duration of this Period [The Tribulation]? I think seven years. If you will follow the line of proof I think this can be made clear. The ninth chapter of Daniel contains a prediction that seventy periods of time, called "weeks," must elapse.... Then follows the announcement that after sixty-nine "weeks" Messiah shall be cut off.... Each of the sixty-nine [prophetic] "weeks" up to the crucifixion was seven years long.... Between the cutting off of Messiah at the end of the sixty-ninth week of Daniel and the taking up of Israel again [the seventieth week], when "the day of vengeance," the Great Tribulation, begins.[3]

As you can see, Scofield makes a statement here that is untrue. He writes, "The taking up of Israel again [the seventieth week], when 'the day of vengeance,' the Great Tribulation, begins." The Bible **never** says the beginning of the seventieth week ("the taking up of Israel again") is "when 'the day of vengeance,' the Great Tribulation, begins." He does rightly state that the seventieth week will be seven years long, as were each of the previous sixty-nine weeks, but that does not mean that the tribulation period within the seventieth week encompasses **all** seven years, especially when the Bible specifically says it does not

(Daniel 12:7, 12).

Rather, Scripture teaches that the initial tribulation begins "in the **middle** of the week . . . [when the Antichrist puts] a stop to sacrifice and grain offering" (Daniel 9:27). In this verse the word "middle" is often interpreted as midpoint, rather than the middle of the seven years which can have a broader range. This was evidenced in ancient Israel when night security guards were posted—they had a first, middle, and last watch (Judges 7:19). The first was from 6 PM to 10 PM, the middle was from 10 PM to 2 AM, and the last was from 2 AM to 6 AM. Therefore, when the first, middle, and last parts of the seventieth week of seven years (a total of 2,556 days) are considered, "the middle of the week" can be any day between the 853rd to the 1,704th day when the Antichrist will break his covenant and abolish the temple sacrifices—starting the end of days tribulation of persecution.

Once the tribulation begins, the Bible says, "from the time that the regular sacrifice is abolished and the abomination of desolation is set up, there will be 1,290 days" (Daniel 12:11). Then, after the abomination of desolation there will be a brief but great tribulation (great persecution) for about forty-five more days. As the Bible says, "Blessed is he who keeps waiting and attains to the 1,335 days!" (Daniel 12:12).

The 1,335 days for the tribulation period are equivalent to "a time, times, and half a time" (Daniel 12:7), or about forty-two months (Revelation 11:2; 13:5), or about three and one-half years (rounded) within the final seven years, the seventieth week. This is the teaching of the Bible regarding the duration of the end of days tribulation period. The modern day dispensationalist teaching that the tribulation is seven years long is not found in Christianity until the early twentieth century—an interpretation that developed with Scofield's seven-year tribulation theory.

## Seven-Year Tribulation Theory

When C.I. Scofield introduced his seven-year tribulation interpretation, it was recognized for what it was—unbiblical. So, it came to be called in the early twentieth century the seven-year tribulation theory.

Nevertheless, Scofield popularized his seven-year tribulation view in the notes of his immensely influential *Scofield Reference Bible* (1909). With his notes alongside sacred text, his seven-year tribulation theory seemed almost divine, thus increasing its acceptability.

According to Gaebelein, by the end of World War II over two million copies of the *Scofield Reference Bible* had sold, and millions have sold since. The *Scofield Reference Bible* persuaded millions of conservative evangelicals to not only believe that the end of days tribulation duration is seven years, but to also believe that its substance includes everything that will occur during the final seven years—from the beginning of birth pains to the terrible wrath of the Lamb judgments of The Revelation.

## SUBSTANCE OF THE TRIBULATION

Scofield's new theory that the end of days tribulation will be seven years long and that it will include the terrible wrath of the Lamb judgments—an awful time when creatures with stings like scorpions torment people for five months (Revelation 9:5,10)—scared the living daylights out of Christians! Tribulation is never a good word, but under Scofield's new definition, Tribulation became a four-headed monster!

Horrified by being told (wrongly) that the end of days tribulation period includes the wrath of the Lamb judgments, frightened evangelicals in droves began to embrace the new pretribulational dispensational premillennialism; the view that the church will be raptured *before* the tribulation.

Thus, Dr. Scofield did not continue with the biblical and historical interpretation of the end of days tribulation that its substance will be, as Hippolytus said, "**the tribulation of the persecution which is to fall upon the church** from the adversary [the Antichrist]."[4] Instead, his seven-year tribulation theory resulted in a reinterpretation of the substance of the tribulation **from** persecution of the church by the Antichrist **to** a four-headed monster tribulation that included the terrible wrath of the Lamb judgments! Consequently, not only did Scofield's theory reinterpret the duration of the tribulation period, it reinterpreted its substance as well.

## THE FATHERS' TEACHINGS ABOUT THE TRIBULATION

Ante-Nicene fathers wrote at length about the end of days tribulation. Irenaeus, the esteemed bishop and theologian of the second century, quotes Scripture and tells about the beginning, the duration, and the substance of the tribulation. He calls it a time when the Antichrist shall reign over the earth:

> For he [the Antichrist] being endued with all the power of the devil, shall come, not as a righteous king ... but an impious, unjust, and lawless one; as an apostate, iniquitous and murderous; as a robber ... and he shall speak words against the most high God, and **wear out the saints** [Christians] of the most high God, and shall purpose to change times and laws; and [everything] shall be given into his hand until **a time, times and a half time,' that is, for three years and six months,** [the tribulation period] during which time, when he comes, he shall reign over the earth.... And then he points out the time that his tyranny shall last, during which the saints shall be put to flight ... 'In the **midst** of the week,' he says, 'the sacrifice and the libation shall be taken away, and the abomination of desolation [shall be brought] into the temple: even unto the consummation of the time.'[5]

Irenaeus says here that during the tribulation period the Antichrist will wear out the saints. Who are the saints? Some people say that the saints refer to Jews. But Paul the apostle wrote to the mostly Gentile church at Corinth calling them saints. He said, "To the church of God which is at Corinth, to those who have been sanctified in Christ Jesus, saints by calling" (1 Corinthians 1:2).

Irenaeus also says here that the Antichrist's tyranny and the end of days tribulation will begin "in the midst [middle] of the week," quoting Daniel 9:27. He says the duration of the tribulation period will be for "a time, times and a half time," quoting Daniel 12:7, or about "three years and six months." He says the substance of the tribulation will include the Antichrist wearing out Christians, "the saints of the most high God," a reference to the persecution of the church. Note also that he says nothing about the end of days tribulation including the wrath of the Lamb judgments of The Revelation.

Hippolytus, the admirable bishop and theologian of the third century, also wrote about the beginning, the duration, and the substance of the end of days tribulation period:

> By mentioning "**a time, and times, and a half,** when the dispersion is accomplished," He indicated the **three years and a half of Antichrist.** For by "a time" he means a year, and by "times" two years, and by a "half a time," half a year. These are the thousand two hundred and ninety [1,290] days of which Daniel prophesied for the finishing of the passion, and the accomplishment of the dispersion when Antichrist comes. In those days they shall know all these things. And **from the time of the removal of the continuous sacrifice** [beginning the tribulation] there are also reckoned one thousand two hundred and ninety days. [Then] iniquity shall abound, as the Lord also says: "Because iniquity shall abound, the love of many shall wax cold." And that divisions will arise when the falling away [apostasy from the Christian faith] takes place, is without doubt. And when divisions arise, love is chilled. The words, "Blessed is he that waiteth and cometh to the **thousand three hundred and five and thirty** [1,335] **days,**" have also their value, as the Lord said: "But he that shall endure unto the end, the same shall be saved."[6]

Hippolytus says here that the tribulation begins "from the time of the removal [stopping or abolishing] of the continuous sacrifice [in the future rebuilt Jerusalem temple]," a reference to Daniel 9:27 that states that this will happen "in the middle [not the midpoint] of the week."

Like Irenaeus, Hippolytus quotes Daniel 12:7 and says the tribulation period duration will be for "a time, and times, and a half" time.

Specifically, he quotes Daniel 12:11 that says there will be 1,290 days from the beginning of the tribulation when the sacrifice is stopped to the abomination of desolation. After this, he cites Daniel 12:12 about the brief great tribulation that follows for another about forty-five days to the 1,335 days (1,290 + 45 = 1,335 days).

Regarding the events of the end of days tribulation, Hippolytus mentions the Antichrist and teaches that during this time there will be a "falling away" from the Christian faith, which Jesus foretold in Matthew 24:10. He also mentions that during the tribulation that "iniquity shall abound, [and] the love of many will wax cold," quoting Matthew 24:12. Still, Hippolytus encourages the church who will endure the end of days tribulation of persecution with the words of Jesus in Mark 13:13 saying, "He that shall endure unto the end, the same shall be saved."

Ante-Nicene father Tatian, a second century theologian and apologist who studied under Justin Martyr, also wrote about the end of days tribulation of persecution, quoting Matthew 24, Luke 21, and Revelation 6:

> There shall be then great tribulation [great persecution], the like of which there hath not been from the beginning of the world till now, nor shall be. And except the Lord had shortened those days, no [Christian] flesh would have lived: but because of the elect, whom he elected, he shortened those days. And there shall be signs in the sun and the moon and the stars; and upon the earth affliction of the nations, and rubbing of hands for the confusion of the noise of the sea. . . . And in those days, straightway after the distress [tribulation] of those days, the sun shall become dark, and the moon shall not shew its light . . . then shall appear the sign of the Son of man [Jesus] in heaven: and at that time all the tribes of the earth shall wail, and look unto the Son of man coming on the clouds of heaven with power and much glory. And he shall send his angels with the great trumpet,

and they shall gather his elect [His church] from the four winds, from one end of heaven [the sky] to the other. But **when these things begin to be, be of good cheer, and lift up your heads; for your salvation is come near.**[7]

Tatian declares here that when the brief but great tribulation of the church begins that it will be accompanied by "signs in the sun and the moon and the stars," quoting Luke 21:25; that those days will be "shortened," quoting Matthew 24:22; and that the sun shall be darkened and "the moon shall not" show its light, quoting Matthew 24:29 and Revelation 6:12. Then, he proclaims will appear Jesus "coming on the clouds of heaven" to "gather his elect," in reference to the resurrection and rapture of the church, "from the four winds, from one end of heaven [the sky] to the other," quoting Matthew 24:30-31.

Early church premillennialists held that the Scriptures later designated as Matthew 24:29-31 is a text on the resurrection and rapture of the church. Although modern dispensational premillennialists interpret Matthew 24:29-31 as pertaining to Armageddon (when Jesus returns to earth), notice that this passage says nothing about Jesus returning to earth at this point; He is only seen in the sky ingathering His elect, the whole company of the redeemed, the church.

Further, modern pretribulational dispensational premillennialists teach that the New Testament texts of Matthew 24, Luke 21, and Revelation 6 do not apply to the church, but to Israel only. However, those who lived closest to the disciples of Jesus Christ—the Ante-Nicene fathers—most certainly did not hold such an interpretation . . . and neither should you!

Like Hippolytus, Tatian also encourages the church who will endure the end of days tribulation of persecution with the words of Jesus in Luke 21:28: "When these things begin to be, be of good cheer, and lift up your heads; for your salvation is come near."

## WHY THE TRIBULATION IS MISUNDERSTOOD TODAY

Dr. C.I. Scofield's widely held seven-year tribulation theory teaches that the duration of the tribulation encompasses **all** seven years of the seventieth week, and that its substance includes the terrible wrath of the Lamb judgments. This misunderstanding of Scripture is false doctrine not found in Christian literature before the twentieth century. This is why the tribulation is misunderstood today.

On the other hand, early church premillennialists taught what the Scriptures plainly teach about the tribulation. They quoted Scripture that teaches that the duration of the tribulation period will be "for a time, times, and half a time" (Daniel 12:7), or about 3 ½ years within the seventieth week, and that its substance will be the Antichrist's persecution of the church. As Hippolytus remarked, "The tribulation of the persecution which is to fall upon the church from the adversary [the Antichrist]."[10]

Now that we have a biblical understanding of the relationship of Israel and the church, of the seventieth week, and of the coming tribulation of persecution which is to fall upon the church from the Antichrist, let's go a step further. Did Jesus tell us of any precursors (signs) that will precede His return and the rapture of the church?

# 7

# Precursors to Christ's Return

Many people today believe Christ's return could happen any moment.

In the early nineteenth century the Baptist minister William Miller was convinced that Jesus Christ would return in the year 1844. But one of his Millerite followers was more specific and predicted that Jesus would return on October 22, 1844. As that day dawned thousands of Millerites stood on hills and housetops waiting eagerly for Christ to return. When the hopeful day passed the Millerites called it a Great Disappointment.

More recently, the pastor and radio evangelist Rev. Harold Camping speculated that Christ would return between September 15 and 27, 1994. After that timeframe passed he predicted with a highly publicized campaign that Christ would return on May 21, 2011, at 6:00 P.M., New Zealand time.

These disappointed followers should have known that Jesus stated clearly that not even He knew the day or hour of His return, "but only the Father" (Matthew 24:36 NIV).

Yet, there is one thing we do know, and that is, Christ will return! As Jesus said, "I will come again and receive you to Myself, that where I am, there you may be also" (John 14:3).

Knowing that Jesus will return, did He reveal any precursors to His coming? Since this question is debated by today's Christian community, you need to know why some leaders teach no biblical precursors to Christ's return, and why other leaders teach biblical precursors to Christ's return.

## NO BIBLICAL PRECURSORS TO CHRIST'S RETURN

When John Darby introduced dispensationalism, along with its eschatology, pretribulational dispensational premillennialism, it included two features: 1) that Israel and the church are two distinct groups—even though the Bible teaches that Jesus has "made both groups into one" (Ephesians 2:14), and 2) the imminent return of Jesus Christ (imminency).

The first feature that Israel and the church are two distinct groups led to the dispensationalist teaching that the church **must** absolutely be removed from the earth by rapture before Israel can resume her dispensational seventieth week, the final seven years.

The second feature of imminency led to the dispensationalist teaching that Christ's return and the rapture of the church could happen "any moment-any second," even though Jesus foretold signs (precursors) to His return—some of which at this writing are not yet fulfilled.

For almost two centuries now the dispensationalist doctrine of Christ's "any moment-any second" return has produced euphoria among believers. However, dispensationalists have found this "any moment-any second" interpretation problematic since some gospel chapters teach precursors. As a result, dispensationalists assert that the New Testament gospel chapters of Matthew 24, Mark 13, and Luke 21—in which Jesus foretold precursors to His return—do **not** apply to the Christian church, but to Israel only.

Consequently, dispensationalists claim that there are **no precursors** to Christ's return applicable to the church, and so teach that a secret coming of Christ and a secret rapture of the church could happen "any moment-any second."

Certainly, everyone should be ready "any moment-any second" to meet the Lord since everyone is only one heartbeat away from eternity. However, Jesus specifically named signs that will precede His return, saying: "When these things [precursors] begin to take place, straighten up and lift up your heads, because your redemption is drawing near" (Luke 21:28).

## BIBLICAL PRECURSORS TO CHRIST'S RETURN

From the early first century believers have consistently held that the Scriptures state precursors to Christ's return and the resurrection and rapture of the church.

### Early Church Teachings

Clement of Rome, who tradition holds was a co-worker with the great apostle Paul and who was appointed bishop of Rome by apostle Peter, presented the first known explanation of precursors to Christ's return. In his First Epistle to the Corinthians, Clement addressed Christians who began doubting that Jesus would return. In doing so, he used an analogy comparing precursors to ripened fruit **to** signs of Christ's return:

> Far from us be that . . . of a doubting heart; who say, "these things we have heard even in the times of our fathers; but, behold, we have grown old, and none of them has happened unto us." Ye foolish ones! Compare yourselves to a tree: take the vine. First of all, it sheds its **leaves**, then it **buds**, next it puts forth **leaves**, and then it **flowers**; after that comes the **sour grape**, and then follows the **ripened fruit**. Ye perceive how in a little time the fruit of a tree comes to maturity. Of a truth, soon and suddenly shall His will be accomplished, as the Scripture also bears witness, saying, "Speedily will He come, and will not tarry;" and, "The Lord shall suddenly come to His temple, even the Holy One, for whom ye look."[1]

In other words, just as there are precursors to ripened fruit, so there are precursors to Christ's return and our gathering to Him by resurrection and rapture.

Cyprian, third century bishop of Carthage, cites precursors to our Lord's return found in Matthew 24 and Luke 21. He reminds his church that adversity will increase in the last times and encourages them with our Lord's promise concerning these things:

> With the exhortation of His foreseeing word, instructing, and teaching, and preparing, and strengthening the people of His church for all endurance of things to come, He predicted and said that wars, and famines, and earthquakes, and pestilences would arise in each place; and lest an unexpected and new dread of mischiefs should shake us, He previously warned us that adversity would increase more and more in the last times. . . . Whatever things were promised will also follow; as the Lord Himself promises, saying, "But when ye see all **these things** [precursors] come to pass, know ye that the kingdom of God is at hand."[2]

Here, Cyprian reiterates the New Testament gospel accounts naming "wars, and famines, and earthquakes, and pestilences" that Jesus foretold will precede His coming again. These adversities that will characterize the end of days should not discourage the follower of Christ. Rather, a Christian can inwardly rejoice, because as Cyprian reminds his church from Luke 21:31, "When ye see all these things come to pass, know ye that the kingdom of God is at hand."

The brilliant early church theologian Tertullian also wrote about precursors to Christ's return, quoting Jesus in Luke's gospel:

> Being questioned by His disciples when those things were to come to pass [**Luke 21**] which He had just been uttering about the destruction of the temple, He discourses to them first of the order of Jewish events until the overthrow of Jerusalem, and then of such as concerned all nations up to the very end of the world. . . . For, says He, "the powers of heaven shall be shaken; and then shall they see the Son of man coming in the clouds, with power and great glory. And when **these things** begin to come to pass, then look up, and lift up your heads, for your redemption draweth nigh." He

spake of its "drawing nigh," not of its being present already; and of "those things beginning to come to pass," not of their having happened: because **when they have come to pass, then** our redemption shall be at hand. . . . He immediately annexes a parable of this in "the trees which are tenderly sprouting into a flower-stalk, and then developing the flower, which is the **precursor** of the fruit." So likewise ye, "when ye shall see all these things [precursors] come to pass, know ye that the kingdom of heaven is nigh at hand."[3]

Tertullian, like Clement of Rome and Cyprian, is quite clear here that there are Scriptural precursors to Christ's return and the rapture of the church. Concerning these things he encourages the church, quoting Jesus in Luke 21:28: "When ye shall see all these things come to pass, know ye that the kingdom of heaven is nigh at hand."

## Modern Church Teachings

Dr. Thomas D. Lea (1938-1999), who served as Dean of Theology at Southwestern Theological Seminary, comments on Ante-Nicene fathers' teaching about Scriptural precursors to Christ's return:

The return of Christ as taught by the Ante-Nicene fathers was an event that occurred after tribulation and persecution of God's people. . . . It is impossible to see how the Ante-Nicene fathers can be described as giving teaching that supports the view of a pretribulational return of Christ. . . . We as Christians must have a sense of expectancy that the return of Christ is an event that can occur quickly in the plan of God. However, we cannot use the teaching of the fathers to support the contention that Christ is coming at any moment. Their view was clearly the idea that He would come **after** a period of tribulation [of persecution] and difficulty for the people of God.[4]

In other words, declares Dr. Lea, there are biblical precursors to

Christ's return, one being that that He will "come after a period of tribulation and difficulty for the people of God," the church.

Reformed theologian Engelsma also names signs that the church should expect before our Lord's return that are foretold in Thessalonians and Matthew 24:

> Expect increasing lawlessness in the world, apostasy from the truth in the churches, the establishment of the kingdom of Antichrist over the entire world. . . . This is the clear, irrefutable teaching of II Thessalonians 2. . . . Opposing Christ, he [the Antichrist] will necessarily oppose Christ's church. This will be great tribulation [great persecution] for the church. . . . Throughout Matthew 24:4-31, Jesus gives instruction to His church concerning the end of the world, and the things which the church must expect.[5]

In addition, Engelsma expresses alarm with three modern prophecy views. His concern with preterism and postmillennialism is that they teach precursors such as the apostasy, the Antichrist, and the tribulation are in the **past**. His worry with pretribulational dispensational premillennialism is that it "bewitches multitudes of supposed evangelicals and fundamentalists so that they expect . . . a secret 'rapture' of the church [before precursors are fulfilled]."[6] Engelsma declares about these teachings that "it leaves the people unprepared for the struggle that lies ahead for the church, the fiercest struggle that the church has ever faced. It renders the people oblivious to the gathering storm at this very moment."[7]

It should be remembered that Jesus foretold precursors to His return—not to frighten us—but to encourage and strengthen His church when these things begin. As Jesus said, "When these things begin to happen, look up and lift up your heads, because your redemption draws near" (Luke 21:28 NKJV).

Jesus also referred to these precursors as birth pains of creation.

# 8

# BIRTH PAINS TO STRIKE THE WORLD

*The whole creation has been groaning*
*as in the pains of childbirth. (Romans 8:22 NIV)*

Just as parents wait in eager expectation for the birth of a child, so also the creation waits for the birth of the children of God by resurrection and rapture into the returning arms of the Great Physician, Jesus Christ. Paul the apostle explains:

> For the creation waits in eager expectation for the **children of God** to be revealed. For the creation was subjected to frustration, not by its own choice, but by the will of the one who subjected it, in hope that the creation itself will be liberated from its bondage to decay and brought into the freedom and glory of the children of God. We know that the whole creation has been groaning as in the **pains of childbirth** right up to the present time. (Romans 8:19-22 NIV)

Toews, in his commentary on *Romans*, clarifies:

> The redemption of creation will be mediated through the glorification of the family of God at the *parousia* [the coming of Christ]. So eager is the intense expectation of creation for this redemption that it is likened to **childbirth**.[1]

Just as women often experience discomfort before childbirth, such as morning sickness and dizziness, so also for thousands of years the creation, figuratively speaking, has been experiencing pains of childbirth such as wars, famines, and earthquakes. Yet, as mothers know, pains of childbirth generally increase as the time to give birth draws near.

Then comes that startling moment that every woman who undergoes natural childbirth encounters — birth pains begin which will end with the birth of their child. Likewise, the creation will experience that startling moment when birth pains begin, which will end with the birth of the children of God (the whole company of the redeemed, the elect, the church). God's Word describes the beginnings of the birth pains and what to expect when they intensify.

## BIRTH PAINS BEGIN

Fortunately, birth pains are temporary and typically have a happy ending, as Campbell relates about creation's birth pains:

> Jesus makes it clear that there are things [precursors] that will happen in the world before his return. These include "wars and rumours of wars . . . famines and earthquakes in various places" (Matthew 24:6–7). These are dislocations in the natural order which Jesus compares to "birth pains" (v. 8; compare Romans 8:22). It is interesting that the comparison is to the pains of a woman giving birth, not to the pains of someone dying. These are birth pangs, not death pangs, and will result in something glorious.[2]

Jesus tells us what will happen when creation's birth pains begin:

> Many will come in my name, claiming, "I am the Christ," and will deceive many. You will hear of wars and rumors of wars, but see to it that you are not alarmed. Such things must happen, but the end is still to come. Nation will rise against nation, and kingdom against kingdom. There will be famines and earthquakes in various places. All these things are the **beginning of birth pains**. (Matthew 24:4-8 NIV)

St. Luke adds: "There will be great earthquakes, and in various places plagues and famines. "(Luke 21:10-11)

In these few verses our Lord names events that will occur when creation's birth pains begin. Specifically, He says there will be false Christs, wars and rumors of wars, famines, great earthquakes, and plagues. Interestingly, four of these birth pains that Jesus names in the gospels mirror the first four seals in chapter six of The Revelation of Jesus Christ to John.

## False Christs

According to tradition, about four hundred people falsely claimed to be the Christ (Greek) or Messiah (Hebrew) prior to Jesus' public ministry. (The devil tries to counterfeit God's work). The same thing will happen before He comes again:

> False Christs and false prophets will arise and will show great
> signs and wonders, so as to mislead, if possible, even the elect.
> Behold, I have told you in advance. (Matthew 24:24-25)

Some of these false Christs will perform great signs and won- ders — miracles — by supernatural satanic power. This is reminiscent of the time when Moses and Aaron stood before Pharaoh. Aaron threw down his staff before Pharaoh and it became a serpent (by God's power). Then Pharaoh called for his sorcerers and they threw down their staffs and they also became serpents (by Satan's power). "But Aaron's staff swallowed up their staffs" (Exodus 7:12).

False Christs already exist today. You may have read about the former IT specialist, Alan John Miller, who runs a religious group in Australia. "'Mr. Miller claims that not only is he Christ, but his partner, Australian Mary Luck, is in fact Mary Magdalene, who according to the Bible was present at the crucifixion. He told Sky News: "I have very clear memories of the crucifixion, but it wasn't as harrowing for me as it was for others like Mary who was present. . . . He also says he remembers performing miracles."'[3]

So far, there is no known record that this imposter has performed miracles, but in time false Christs will. So, do not be deceived by miracles. Instead, test a messenger's message by the Bible. The truth of God's Word and the indwelling Holy Spirit will keep true believers in Jesus from being deceived by false Christs.

Of course, the greatest imposter of all will be the ultimate false Christ—the Antichrist. The Antichrist will claim to be Christ, and will deny Jesus. As St. John wrote:

> Who is the liar but the one who denies that Jesus is the Christ? This is the antichrist, the one who denies the Father and the Son. (1 John 2:22)

Because of great miracles that the Antichrist will perform, many people will be deceived by him. Jesus warns:

> If anyone says to you, "Behold, here is the Christ," or "There He is," do not believe him.... So if they say to you, "Behold, He is in the wilderness," do not go out, or, "Behold, He is in the inner rooms," do not believe them. For just as the lightning comes from the east and flashes even to the west, so will the coming of the Son of Man be. (Matthew 24:23,26,27)

Ante-Nicene father Tatian adds:

> If any man say unto you, the Messiah is here; or, Lo, he is there; believe him not. There shall rise then false Messiahs [false Christs] and prophets of lying, and shall do signs and wonders, in order that they may lead astray even the elect also, if they be able.[4]

When Jesus Christ returns, the whole world will know it! When Jesus comes "on the clouds of the sky with power and great glory" (Matthew 24:30), "every eye will see Him" (Revelation 1:7). So, when creation's birth pains begin, do not be deceived by false Christs.

## Wars and Rumors of Wars

According to *Wars in the World Daily News* there are at this writing sixty countries involved in wars, and three hundred and ninety-five conflicts involving militias-guerrillas, drug cartels, separatist groups, and anarchist groups. In other words, you don't have to go far to find a fight. This is how it will be when creation's birth pains begin, as Jesus said:

> You will be hearing of wars and rumors of wars. See that you are not frightened, for those things must take place, but that is not yet the end. For nation will rise against nation, and kingdom against kingdom. (Matthew 24:6-7)

During the initial birth pains the imposter Christ — the Antichrist — will be a major contributor to war in the world. At the opening of the first seal in Revelation 6 John foretells that the Antichrist will go out "conquering, and to conquer" (v. 6:2). At the opening of the second seal the extent of war is foretold: "It was granted to take peace from the earth, and that men should slay one another" (Revelation 6:4).

Ante-Nicene father Victorinus held that the seals in Revelation 6 mirror the gospel accounts about the birth pains. He comments about the second seal, its rider on the red horse, and the coming wars:

> "And when He had opened the second seal, I heard the second living creature saying, come and see. And there went out another horse that was red, and to him that sat upon him was given a great sword." The red horse, and he that sat upon him, having a sword, signify the coming wars, as we read in the **Gospel**: "For nation shall rise against nation, and kingdom against kingdom."[5]

## Famines

Do you think food prices are high now? Just wait. When creation's birth pains begin, famine will make food scarce. Jesus said, "There will be famines . . . in various places" (Matthew 24:7 NIV).

Historically, one of the most tragic famines was the Great Famine of 1315-1322 that struck Europe, causing millions of deaths. Normally, famine is associated with drought. But in early fourteenth century Europe, it was just the opposite:

> In the spring of 1315, unusually heavy rain began in much of Europe. Throughout the spring and summer, it continued to rain and the temperature remained cool. Under these conditions grain could not ripen.... The price of food began to rise..... Wheat prices increased by 320 percent and peasants could no longer afford bread.... While the Black Death (1338–1375) would kill more, for many the Great Famine was worse. While the plague swept through an area in a matter of months, the Great Famine lingered for years, drawing out the suffering of those who would slowly starve to death.[6]

During the Great Famine the dreadful byproducts of famine were "extreme levels of criminal activity [people stealing food to survive], disease and mass death, infanticide, and cannibalism."[7]

In the last century, famines in Asia, Africa, and the former Soviet Union claimed the lives of an estimated seventy million people.[8] More recently, in the American Midwest one of the worst droughts since the 1950's withered crops across the bread basket states, causing one farmer to opine, "No crops means no feed for livestock.... In the end this will lead to increased food prices."[9]

When creation's birth pains begin, our Lord forecasts in The Revelation at the opening of the third seal what will be the cost of food: "A quart of wheat for a denarius (a day's wages), and three quarts of barley for a denarius" (v. 6:6). Working all day just for a jar of wheat is a high price for food.

Victorinus comments on the third seal of Revelation 6 and the birth pain of famine:

> "And when He had opened the third seal. I heard the third

living creature saying, come and see. And, lo, a black horse; and he who sat upon it had a balance in his hand." The black horse signifies famine, for the Lord says, "There shall be famines in divers places;" but the word is specially extended to the times of Antichrist, when there shall be a great famine.[10]

During the Great Famine in which millions perished because they could no longer afford food, or if they had the means could no longer find food, were any of them born-again Christians? Probably. In America's Bible Belt states struck by drought that withered crops across the Midwest adversely affecting tens of thousands of people, were any of them born-again Christians? Indeed, yes. The point is: Our Lord has told His church in advance about the coming famine. So, we should take a lesson from the ant who in summer prepares her food for the winter (Proverbs 30:25).

## Great Earthquakes

Have you done the Shake, Rattle 'n Roll, lately? If not, hang on. Your time is coming. Jesus said, "There will be great earthquakes" (Luke 21:10-11).

R. Webb has researched earthquake trends and compiled in March 2011 a detailed report. In this report he includes a graph showing how the number of all magnitude earthquakes has escalated six-fold since 1973. However, he notes that this trend for all magnitude earthquakes should be understood in relation to the increased number of seismograph stations around the world, enabling lower intensity earthquakes to be noticed in recent decades that may have gone undetected in earlier periods.

For this reason, Webb's report primarily concerns long term trends of larger magnitude 7.0 or above — great earthquakes — that he says are easily detected with fewer seismograph stations. Webb says that records for these major earthquakes are fairly good from the 1880s on, yet he places more assurance in global earthquake data after 1901. Therefore, based on data from the U.S. Geological Survey (USGS) and other sources for great earthquakes magnitude 7.0 or above since

1901, his findings are: Years 1901 to 1938 (38 years) 53 Mag. 7.0> earthquakes; Years 1939 to 1976 (38 years) 71 Mag. 7.0> earthquakes; and Years 1977 to 2014 (38 years) 164 Mag. 7.0> earthquakes as of March 2011 and predicts >190 Mag. 7.0 earthquakes by 2014.

Although his research indicates a more than doubling in the number of great earthquakes in the recent period compared to the prior period, it is trends in recent years that are startling, as Webb explains:

> Between 1986 and 1996 (inclusive), a period of eleven years, there were "just" **fifteen** earthquakes listed by USGS of magnitude 7.0 or greater. . . . But between 1997 and 2007 (inclusive), a period of only eleven years, there were **ninety-nine** earthquakes with magnitude 7.0 or greater. This is more than a six-fold increase on the previous similar period, and is a stark increase on any earlier decades in the twentieth century.[11]

With the realization of such a marked increase in recent years in great earthquakes, Webb comments:

> Jesus is quoted as saying "in various places there will be famines and earthquakes—these things are the beginning of birth pangs"(ref: Matthew 24). Now, because birth pains begin small and then increase in intensity and frequency, this passage can be interpreted to mean that earthquakes . . . will increase both in frequency and impact/strength prior to Jesus' second coming. Although Jesus is clear that no one will know the day or the hour, and his return will indeed happen "when you do not expect," he does give us broad pointers, one of these being natural events—like earthquakes.[12]

Some may discount biblical signs of Christ's return, such as the Jews returning to their homeland and the proliferation of wars, but a six-fold increase in recent years in magnitude 7.0 or above great earthquakes is undeniable handwriting on the wall.

Ante-Nicene father Hippolytus comments about earthquakes during the birth pains:

> And what am I to say with respect to men, when the very elements themselves will disown their order? There will be earthquakes in every city.[13]

When creation's birth pains begin you'll hear breaking news of metropolitan areas devastated by earthquakes. Creation will be groaning to give birth to the children of God—the church—by resurrection and rapture at Christ's return.

Cyprian encouraged his church to endure earthquakes and other predicted birth pains:

> Preparing, and strengthening the people of His church for all endurance of things to come, He [the Lord] predicted and said that wars, and famines, and earthquakes, and pestilences would arise in each place.... He previously warned us that adversity would increase more and more in the last times . . . saying, "But when ye see all these things come to pass, know ye that the kingdom of God is at hand."[14]

## Plagues

Jesus said there will be "in various places plagues" (Luke 21:11). Plagues may occur as a consequence of war, famine, or great earthquakes.

The most notorious was the Black Plague or Black Death during the middle fourteenth century:

> Today, scientists understand that the Black Death, now known as the plague, is spread by a bacillus called Yersina pestis ["Human Y. pestis infection takes three main forms: pneumonic, septicemic, and the infamous bubonic plaques."[15]].... They know that the bacillus travels from person to person pneumonically, or through the air, as well as through the bite of infected fleas and rats. Both of these pests could be found almost everywhere in medieval

Europe, but they were particularly at home aboard ships of all kinds—which is how the deadly plague made its way through one European port city after another.... In a panic, healthy people did all they could to avoid the sick. Doctors refused to see patients; priests refused to administer last rites. Shopkeepers closed stores. Many people fled the cities for the countryside, but even there they could not escape the disease: It affected cows, sheep, goats, pigs and chickens as well as people.[16]

The Black Plague killed an estimated 200 million people,[17] reducing the world's population at the time by an estimated ten percent. According to the World Health Organization, Black Plague continues to kill about 3,000 people each year.

In the sixth chapter of Revelation, the first five seals mirror our Lord's account in Matthew 24 of creation's birth pains. At the fourth seal it is prophesied that authority will be given "over a fourth of the earth to kill by sword [war], famine and plague" (Revelation 6:8 NIV). One interpretation of this verse is that a fourth of the world's population (about two billion people) will perish. Just as the number of fatalities during the fourteenth century Great Famine and Black Plague was incredible, so will the number of fatalities from war, famine and plague during creation's birth pains be incredible. Hippolytus says, "There will be ... plagues in every country."[18]

Plagues, great earthquakes, famines, wars and rumors of wars, and false Christs are man-made and natural disasters that our Lord figuratively described as "the beginning of birth pains" (Matthew 24:8 NIV). Yet, typically birth pains increase in frequency and intensity. The Bible tells us what will happen when creation's birth pains intensify.

## BIRTH PAINS INTENSIFY

Suddenly, the room became hot. Then dizziness ... and the room started to spin! That's when I knew that I had better sit down—quickly—before I fainted.

My wife, Susan, was in labor with our first child and her birth pains had grown intense. As her breathing became more rapid, as she pushed and groaned, as her hand locked down on mine with the grip of an iron vise, and as she screamed and struggled to give birth it almost caused me to faint. And I had the easy job. (Of course, I was too manly to admit that I was about to collapse). Indeed, birth pains can be challenging, especially when they intensify. Still, as birth pains intensify there is the realization that birth is near.

Likewise, when creation's birth pains intensify there will be the realization among insightful believers that birth of the children of God who will be caught away to meet the Lord in the air, is near. Yet, between now and then the creation (to include the church metaphorically described in Revelation 19:7 as a woman) will suffer intense birth pains to include extreme weather; terrors; supernatural signs in the sun, moon, and stars; distress of nations; and lawlessness—all of which will end gloriously with the birth of the church, the elect, the whole company of the redeemed by resurrection and rapture into the returning arms of our great God and Savior, Jesus Christ.

## Extreme Weather

As birth pains intensify Jesus predicted that weather conditions will become even more extreme, leading to the roaring of the sea and great storms. He foretold, "There will be . . . perplexity at the roaring of the sea and the waves, men fainting from fear" (Luke 21:25-26).

These unusual conditions appear to be taking shape based on a *New York Times* report on "weather extremes that are growing more frequent and intense:"[19]

> China is enduring its coldest winter in nearly 30 years. Brazil is in the grip of a dreadful heat spell. Eastern Russia is so freezing—minus 50 degrees Fahrenheit, and counting—that the traffic lights recently stopped working in the city of Yakutsk. . . . "Each year we have **extreme weather**, but it's unusual to have so many extreme events around the world at once," said Omar Baddour, chief of the data management applications division at the World Meteorological

Organization, in Geneva. . . . Such events are **increasing in intensity as well as frequency,** Mr. Baddour said. . . . To the north, the extremes have swung the other way . . . In Inner Mongolia, 180,000 livestock froze to death. The cold has wreaked havoc with crops, sending the price of vegetables soaring. . . . "The intensity of the cold is unusual," Mr. Lynn said. "It seems the weather is going to become more intense; there's going to be more extremes."[20]

Strong storms are also increasing in frequency and intensity. At this writing it is reported that a tornado in Oklahoma was the widest in history.[21] In central Europe torrential rains have caused the worst flooding in five centuries.[22] And brace for more hurricanes. In a study led by James Elsner of Florida State University, his team "looked at hurricane data from across the world between 1981 and 2006. They published their data in the scientific journal *Nature* in 2008. They found a 31 percent increase."[23]

Hippolytus wrote about strong storms that will occur during the birth pains:

> Storms of winds will disturb both sea and land excessively; and there will be unfruitfulness on the earth, and a roaring in the sea . . . intemperateness in the atmosphere, discharges of hail upon the face of the earth, winters of excessive severity, different frosts, inexorable scorching winds.[24]

As birth pains intensify, expect the extreme weather to affect crop production, and will cause off-the-charts strong storms. These breaking news strong storms will cause people "perplexity at the roaring of the sea and the waves, men fainting from fear and the expectation of the things which are coming upon the world" (Luke 21:25-26).

### Terrors

Exploding with an atmospheric impact of some 20-30 times more energy than released by the Hiroshima atomic bomb, was the recent

Chelyabinsk Super bolide Meteor. This object raced across the Russian sky injuring about 1,500 people, and creating a shockwave that shattered glass in about 7,200 buildings in six cities.[25] This meteor fits the description foretold by Jesus: "There will be ... terrors [Gk., *phóbētron;* fearful sights, terrors]" (Luke 21:11). *The New International Greek Testament Commentary* adds about these terrors:

> Luke ... suggests that climactic events are in view ... but the context suggests a broader meaning, "in place after place" ... on earth.[26]

When terrors come the Lord's people are not to fear says the Psalmist: "You will not fear the terror of night. . . . A thousand may fall at your side, ten thousand at your right hand, but it will not come near you" (Psalm 91:5,7 NIV).

## Supernatural Signs in the Sun, Moon, and Stars

"There will be signs in the sun, moon and stars," Jesus said (Luke 21:25 NIV).

Ancient people looked to the stars for signs foreshadowing human events. One anticipated event was the birth of the King of the Jews, the Messiah. About Him it was prophesied that "a star shall come forth out of Jacob, and a scepter shall rise out of Israel" (Numbers 24:17 RSV), and "nations will come to your light, and kings to the brightness of your rising" (Isaiah 60:3).

The wise men, called magi, knew about these prophecies. Herodotus, a fifth century Greek historian, mentions "magi" as "a priestly caste of Media or Persia" who believed the affairs of history were reflected in the movements of the stars. Because of their insight into astronomy, rulers of the East commonly inquired of them to determine affairs of state.

While observing the stars the magi saw a sign—a "star in the east"—that they identified as heralding the birth of the King of the Jews, and following the star they came to Jerusalem and then to Bethlehem and worshiped the baby Jesus.

A common explanation for the star, often called the Bethlehem Star, is that it "would not have been a star at all, but rather a conjunction of the planets Jupiter and Saturn in the constellation Pisces in 7 B.C., having the appearance of a great star."[27] Yet, this explanation is inconsistent with the biblical account that says, "The star, which they had seen in the east, went on before them until it came and stood over the place where the Child was" (Matthew 2:9). In other words, there was a beam of light from a star that guided them, or as Matthew 2:9 says, "went on before them until it came and stood over the place where" was laid baby Jesus. Therefore, the star was a supernatural sign.

When Jesus came the first time—accompanied by a supernatural sign in the sky—He came to "save His people from their sins" (Matthew 1:21). When He comes the "second time, not to bear sin, but to bring salvation to those who are waiting for him" (Hebrews 9:28), His return will be preceded by supernatural "signs in the sun, moon and stars" (Luke 21:25 NIV). These celestial warnings will include the sun turning "black like sackcloth" and the moon turning "blood red" (Revelation 6:12 NIV). Also, "the sun will be darkened, and the moon will not give its light ... and they will see the Son of Man coming on the clouds of the sky" (Matthew 24:29-30).

## Distress of Nations

Jesus said, "There will be ... distress of nations" (Luke 21:25 NIV). As creation's birth pains intensify there will be increasing severity of natural and man-made disasters that will cause people and entire nations to be in distress. *The Pulpit Commentary* remarks:

> Our Lord indicates that distress of nations, perplexity, and faint-heartedness through fear will precede his ... coming. But his people need be no sharers in this fear. So far from this ... they are to lift up their heads, assured that redemption is drawing nigh [Luke 21:28]. The outlook may be wintry for the world, but it is summer for the saints of God. ... There need be no fear. Let this be left to the unbelieving world.[28]

## Lawlessness

Have you dreamed about vacationing in Brazil? Known for its spectacular beaches and its love for football (soccer), Brazil has been chosen to host the Olympics. Yet, did you know that Brazil is ranked number six among the most dangerous countries. "Beneath all the hype about what a great tourist spot Brazil is lies a crime rate that is absurdly high, with murder rates reaching as much as 40,000 deaths annually. Robberies, kidnapping, and other criminal activities are also rampant."[29]

Are you considering a sales trip in America? You might ask for hazard pay if you go to these cities: Detroit, Memphis, Miami, Las Vegas, and Stockton, California. They are ranked the top five most dangerous.[30] Also, if you are expecting mail you might have a long wait in Brooklyn. According to the New York Post, "Postmen are too scared to deliver letters and packages to one of Brooklyn's most crime-ravaged neighborhoods."[31]

Still, the western world is relatively tame compared to parts of Africa and the Middle East. One Travel & Leisure magazine writer quips: "If tomorrow morning Africa and the Middle East simply vanished, you have to wonder what would happen to the State Department functionaries who write the travel warnings at travel.state.gov. The poor people would have little to do all day. . . . Political unrest, rebel roadblocks, street crime—the warnings are as plentiful as they are disturbing."[32]

As creation's birth pains intensify, so will lawlessness. People will become distrustful and cold toward others. Jesus said, "Because lawlessness will abound, the love of many will grow cold" (Matthew 24:12 NKJV).

Jesus also said that when He returns that conditions "will be just like the days of Noah" (Matthew 24:37). In those days "the earth was filled with violence [lawlessness]" (Genesis 6:11). Not surprising, though, the most lawless person during the birth pains will be the Antichrist, as Paul the apostle explains:

With regard to the coming of our Lord Jesus Christ and our

> gathering together to Him ... let no one in any way deceive
> you, for it will not come unless the apostasy comes first, and
> the **man of lawlessness** [the Antichrist] is revealed, the son
> of destruction, who opposes and exalts himself above every
> so-called god or object of worship, so that he takes his seat
> in the temple of God, displaying himself as being God. (2
> Thessalonians 2:1,3,4)

The lawless actions of the Antichrist, the deceptive sensationalism of other false Christs, and the effects of wars and rumors of wars, famines, great earthquakes, plagues, extreme weather, terrors, supernatural signs, distress of nations, and lawlessness will bring shocking news when birth pains strike the world.

Further, the Antichrist's lawless actions inflicted on Christians will bring distress analogous to birth pains upon the church.

As Paul said, "The whole creation has been groaning as in the pains of childbirth" (Romans 8:22 NIV). Let us remember that the church—the children of God—is the "baby" that will exit the womb of the earth, figuratively speaking, when creation gives birth to the children of God by resurrection and rapture into the open arms of the Great Physician, Jesus Christ, at His return. Just as a baby experiences distress passing through the narrow birth canal during a woman's intense birth pains (hard labor), so will the children of God experience distress when the Antichrist's actions analogous to birth pains strike the church!

# 9

# BIRTH PAINS TO STRIKE THE CHURCH

*"Then they will deliver you to tribulation (Gk., thlípsis; tribulation, persecution, distress, affliction, anguish), and will kill you, and you will be hated by all nations because of My name"*

*- (Matthew 24:9)*

Renowned early church bishop, theologian, and Ante-Nicene father Hippolytus in his *Treatise on Christ and the Antichrist* wrote about the birth pains to strike the church calling it "the tribulation of the persecution which is to fall upon the church from the adversary [the Antichrist]."[1]

Although waves of tribulation that were generally isolated to countries, regions, or an empire have struck the Christian church before, this last end of days tribulation will be the most widespread in history. It will be global. As Jesus said, "You will be hated by **all** nations because of My name" (Matthew 24:9).

Since every Christian on earth will experience the tribulation of the persecution which is to fall upon the church from the Antichrist, this chapter will prepare you with an explanation about tribulation and its benefits for the believer and with the consequences of the end of days tribulation of persecution.

## TRIBULATION AND ITS BENEFITS FOR THE BELIEVER

Most Christians agree with biblical teaching about tribulation as presented here by *The Complete Word Study Dictionary: New Testament*:

> Tribulation is the appointed destiny of Christians. Paul reminds the Thessalonians that both he and they were appointed unto tribulation and that he had told them before that they were to suffer tribulation (1 Thess. 3:3f.). John is also a partaker in the "tribulation and kingdom and patience which are in Jesus" (a.t. [Rev. 1:9]); and he tells the church of Smyrna that they shall suffer tribulation ten days (Rev. 2:10). "Through many tribulations we must enter into the kingdom of God" (a.t. [Acts 14:22]).... "Our light tribulation, which is for the moment, worketh for us more and more exceedingly an eternal weight of glory" (a.t. [2 Cor. 4:17]). "Tribulation worketh patience" (Rom. 5:3 [cf. Rev. 1:9]). God comforts the faithful in tribulation (2 Cor. 1:4; 7:6), and the comfort thus given enables them to comfort others (2 Cor. 1:4). His judgment will put an end to their tribulation, and they will be rewarded with rest (2 Thess. 1:5ff. [cf. Rev. 2:10]).[2]

The *New Bible Commentary* adds:

> The tribulation of the people of Christ is in some sense a participation in the sufferings of Christ (Col. 1:24; cf. 2 Cor. 1:5; 4:10f.; Phil. 3:10; 1 Pet. 4:13).... The tribulations of the people of Christ are instrumental in promoting their moral transformation into the likeness of Christ (Rom. 5:3f.; 2 Cor. 3:18 with 4:8–12, 16f.).[3]

Thus, tribulation, as painful as it may be and as strange as it may seem, produces a number of positive benefits in a believer's life. It works patience, it brings an eternal weight of glory, and it helps transform a Christian into the likeness of Christ. This is what the Bible teaches about tribulation and its benefits for the believer—spiritual and eternal benefits—that derive from frequent tribulation challenges of following Christ in a fallen world and that will derive from following Christ during the end of days tribulation of persecution "which is to fall upon the church from the adversary [the Antichrist].⁴

## CONSEQUENCES OF THE TRIBULATION OF PERSECUTION

Last words are often profound. Some of the last words Jesus spoke during His final days before the cross were concerning the end of days tribulation of persecution. When asked, "What will be the sign of Your coming, and of the end of the age?" (Matthew 24:3), what was His reply? He described imprisonment, persecution and martyrdom, betrayal, apostasy, an abomination of desolation, a great tribulation, and that the gospel will be preached to the whole world. Subsequently, in the Revelation of Jesus Christ to John, He revealed economic war against the church (Revelation 13: 16-17).

### Imprisonment

Jesus said, "They will deliver you to synagogues and prisons, and you will be brought before kings and governors, and all on account of my name" (Luke 21:12 NIV).

Being arrested for witnessing about salvation in Jesus Christ would never happen in America, right? Think again. Not too long ago, four Christians in Dearborn, Michigan, were arrested for sharing the gospel:

Michigan state Rep. Tom McMillin called on the state attorney general to investigate the arrests, saying the Christians were just "engaging festivalgoers in conversation about religion on public property." . . . One witness named Steven Atkins, a resident of Toronto, Canada, said, "I never thought I would see this in America. . . . I heard people clapping and applauding, and some said 'Allahu akbar,'" he said. "It was an intense discussion, but it was not unruly." . . . Robert

> Muise, senior trial counsel . . . told Detroit's WDIV-TV 4,
> "If people are offended by the fact that they were preaching
> the Gospel of Jesus Christ to Muslims and trying to convert
> Muslims, well, guess what: We have a First Amendment."[5]

Jesus told His followers: "Whenever you are arrested and brought to trial, do not worry beforehand about what to say. Just say whatever is given you at the time, for it is not you speaking, but the Holy Spirit" (Mark 13:11 NIV). Such an occasion will give you an opportunity to share your Christian testimony. As Jesus says, "It will lead to an opportunity for your testimony. So make up your minds not to prepare beforehand to defend yourselves; for I will give you utterance and wisdom which none of your opponents will be able to resist or refute" (Luke 21:13-15).

## Persecution and Martyrdom

Jesus said, "They will lay their hands on you and will persecute you" (Luke 21:12).

Like all other birth pains, Christian persecution is also increasing around the world in frequency and intensity. In Muslim countries "millions of Christians are being displaced from one end of the Islamic world to the other" writes Raymond Ibrahim, author of *Crucified Again: Exposing Islam's New War on Christians.*[6] "The flight of Christians out of the region is unprecedented and it's increasing year by year"[7] says Leonard Leo, chairman of the U.S. Commission on International Religious Freedom. "In Ethiopia, after a Christian was accused of desecrating a Koran, thousands of Christians were forced to flee their homes when Muslim extremists set fire to roughly fifty churches and dozens of Christian homes. In the Ivory Coast—where Christians have literally been crucified—Islamic rebels massacred hundreds and displaced tens of thousands of Christians."[8]

During the end of days tribulation, Christian persecution will intensify to the point that followers of Jesus Christ "will be hated by all nations" (Matthew 24:9). This worldwide animosity toward Christians will trigger mass martyrdom. As Jesus forewarned, "They will deliver you to tribulation, and will kill you" (Matthew 24:9) This global Christian martyrdom will bring about the prayers of the martyrs, as St. John relates at the opening of the fifth seal of The Revelation:

> When the Lamb opened the fifth seal, I saw under the altar the souls of those who had been killed because they were faithful to the word of God and to the message they had received. These souls shouted in a loud voice, "Holy and true Lord, how long until you judge the people of the earth and punish them for killing us?" Then each one of them was given a white robe and was told to wait a short time longer. There were still some of their fellow servants and brothers and sisters in the service of Christ who must be killed as they were. They had to wait until all of this was finished. (Revelation 6:9-11 NCV)

Remember the words of Jesus:

> My friends, do not be afraid of those who kill the body and after that have no more that they can do. But I will warn you whom to fear: fear the One who, after He has killed, has authority to cast into hell; yes, I tell you, fear Him! (Luke 12:4-5)

Here, the Lord tells His followers that the ungodly can kill the body, but not the soul.

Even though Christian persecution and martyrdom is cruel, our Lord wants us to forgive our persecutors just as Jesus forgave those who persecuted Him. We should also pray that they will repent and turn to follow Jesus Christ as their Savior and Lord so they will be forgiven, saved, and receive eternal life. Further, Christ encourages His followers to endure persecution saying "the one who endures to the end, he will be saved" (Matthew 24:13).

### Betrayal

"The worst pain in the world goes beyond the physical. Even further beyond any other emotional pain one can feel. It is the betrayal of a friend,"[9] writes author Heather Brewer.

Betrayal was felt by a Syrian teenage Christian girl whose neighbors whom she thought were friends turned against her family. Jihadist rebels were targeting secular president Assad, but they were also targeting Syrian Christians for kidnapping and beheadings. The girl said: "We left because they were trying to kill us . . . because we were Christians. . . . Those who were our neighbors turned against us."[10]

Christians in Mali have been betrayed by relatives. "In Mali, after a 2012 Islamic coup, as many as 200,000 Christians fled. . . . There have been house to house searches for Christians who might be in hiding, churches and other Christian property have been looted or destroyed, and people tortured into revealing any Christian relatives."[11] Just as Jesus was betrayed by Judas, so during the tribulation you can expect to be betrayed. As Jesus said:

> You will be betrayed even by parents and brothers and relatives and friends, and they will put some of you to death. (Luke 21:16-17)

Our Lord also said, "Brother will betray brother to death, and a father his child; and children will rise up against parents and have them put to death. You will be hated by all because of My name, but the one who endures to the end, he will be saved" (Mark 13:12-13).

### Economic War against the Church

Not too long ago, the former communist Soviet Union's atheistic policies prohibited Christians from holding political office, depriving them economically.[12] During Roman Emperor Diocletian's Great Persecution, Christians could not hold a government position. Economic war against the church is nothing new.

During the tribulation of persecution, economic war against the church will be imposed worldwide. A mark imprinted on a person's right hand or forehead—signifying their allegiance to the beast, the Antichrist—will be required to perform a financial transaction:

> He required everyone—small and great, rich and poor, free and slave—to be given a mark on the right hand or on the forehead. And no one could buy or sell anything without that mark, which was either the name of the beast or the number representing his name. (Revelation 13:16-17 NLT)

The *New Bible Commentary* remarks:

> The immediate effect of demanding that all receive the mark of the beast is the social ostracism of those who refuse it, and it entails economic warfare by the state against the church.[13]

There has been much speculation about this beast imposed "mark." In ancient times slaves and soldiers were marked by branding or tattooing; similar to the modern practice of cattle branding with a mark that identifies them with their owner, with Beale adding:

> If branding of slaves is in mind here, then the beast's worshipers are seen as his property. If branding of soldiers or of religious devotees is in view, the worshipers are seen as his faithful followers.[14]

The latter seems to be the case, based on our Lord's strong denunciation in Revelation 14:9-10 of anyone taking the mark of the beast, it will signify that a person is a follower of the Antichrist.

In addition, St. John says the mark will contain "either the name of the beast or the number of his name" (Revelation 13:17). In other words, the mark will probably contain data. Hence, one explanation for the mark of the beast is that it may be a barcode used in industry like this QR Code:

If you were apostle John living in the first century and saw in a vision a barcode on someone's hand or forehead, what would you think it was? A mark, maybe?

Interestingly, fifty years ago tattoos were considered taboo and were largely only worn by sailors and rough characters. Today, tattoos are commonplace, a condition which will make it easy for people to accept the mark of the beast.

Whatever form the mark of the beast takes is uncertain, but the important thing to remember is that you **MUST NOT** take it because God's Word says:

> If anyone worships the beast and his image, and receives a mark on his forehead or upon his hand, he also will drink of the wine of the wrath of God ... and he will be **tormented** with fire and brimstone ... forever and ever ... whoever receives the mark of his name. Here is the **perseverance of the saints who keep the commandments of God and their faith in Jesus**. (Revelation 14:9-12)

Sadly, though, millions of Christians today are being misled by a false doctrine into believing that they will be raptured before the Antichrist comes on the scene, before the tribulation, and before the mark of the beast policy is implemented. In essence, Christians are being taught that they will be raptured before anything bad happens.

Consequently, when the tribulation of persecution begins and the Antichrist is demanding that everyone take the mark of the beast or not be able to perform financial transactions, they will be unprepared and will be at risk of taking the mark of the beast and falling away from the Christian faith into apostasy.

## Apostasy

Third century Christians in North Africa had not experienced persecution for many years. Comfortable and content, when the Decian (Roman Emperor Decius) persecution became severe, "many Christians fell away."[15]

During the end of days tribulation this pattern will repeat itself. Jesus said, "At that time many will fall away" (Matthew 24:10). Paul explains that this mass apostasy from the Christian faith will precede the resurrection and rapture of the church—"our gathering together to Him:"

> With regard to the coming of our Lord Jesus Christ and our **gathering together** to Him ... let no one in any way deceive you, for it will not come unless the apostasy comes first, and the man of lawlessness [the Antichrist] is revealed, the son of destruction, who opposes and exalts himself above every so-called god or object of worship, so that he takes his seat in the temple of God, displaying himself as being God. (2 Thessalonians 2:1,3,4)

The Bible is clear here that our gathering to Christ —the resurrection and rapture of the church — will not occur until the Antichrist is revealed and he takes his seat in the rebuilt Jerusalem temple declaring himself God which is the abomination of desolation that will be followed by a great tribulation of persecution (Matthew 24:15,21).

Just as the persecution of Christians in the third century was severe, so will the end of days tribulation of persecution be severe causing many to fall away from the faith—commit apostasy—to their eternal detriment. However, Ante-Nicene father Cyprian encourages the church in such a time to be in "continual prayer and supplication that we fall not away from the heavenly kingdom."[16]

## Abomination of Desolation

Daniel said, "From the time that the regular sacrifice is abolished [starting the tribulation] and the abomination of desolation is set up, there will be 1,290 days" (v. 12:11).

On the 1,290th day after the sacrifices in the rebuilt Jerusalem temple are abolished, the Antichrist will take "his seat in the temple of God, displaying himself as being God" (2 Thessalonians 2:4). Likely, all major television networks will broadcast this pompous ceremony—an occasion celebrated around the world by the decadent and the devils. The great early church writer on prophecy, Hippolytus, encourages the church when this abomination of desolation happens:

> The abomination of desolation being manifested then . . . and the whole world finally approaching the consummation, **what remains but the coming of our Lord and Saviour Jesus Christ** from heaven, for whom we have looked in hope? Who shall bring the conflagration and just judgment upon all who have refused to believe on Him. For the Lord says, "And when these things begin to come to pass, then look up, and lift up your heads; for **your redemption draweth nigh**."[17]

The abomination of desolation will be the occasion when the Antichrist will attempt to annihilate every person on earth that does not worship him—bringing great tribulation on the church. But fortunately, the great tribulation of persecution will be short-lived.

## Great Tribulation of Persecution

If you're near Jerusalem, Scripture says, "you must flee to the mountains" to escape because the Antichrist and his henchmen are nearby. As Jesus warned:

> When you see the abomination of desolation which was spoken of through Daniel the prophet, standing in the holy place (let the reader understand), then those who are in Judea must flee to the mountains. . . . For then there will be a **great**

**tribulation** [great persecution], such as has not occurred since the beginning of the world until now, nor ever will. Unless those days had been cut short, no [Christian] life would have been saved; but for the sake of the elect those days will be **cut short**. (Matthew 24:15,16,21,22)

The approximate duration of the great tribulation of persecution was revealed to Old Testament prophet Daniel. He says, "Blessed is he who waits and attains to the 1,335 days!" (Daniel 12:12). Hippolytus comments:

"Blessed is he that waiteth, and cometh to the thousand three hundred and five and thirty days [1,335 days];" for when the abomination cometh and makes war upon the saints, whosoever shall survive his days, and reach the forty-five days [45 days], . . . to him the kingdom of heaven comes.[18]

In other words, according to the Scriptures there will be about forty-five days of great tribulation (1,290 days of initial tribulation + about 45 days of great tribulation = 1,335 days). However, the actual number of days of great tribulation is unknown because Jesus said "those days will be cut short" (Matthew 24:22).

Once again, early church bishop Hippolytus encourages the church when the brief but great tribulation of persecution happens:

The words, "Blessed is he that waiteth and cometh to the thousand three hundred and five and thirty days [1,335 days]," have also their value, as the Lord said: "But he that shall endure unto the end, the same shall be saved."[19]

Christ's church should not forget during the great tribulation that our "momentary, light affliction (Gk., *thlípsis*; distress, tribulation, persecution, **affliction**, anguish) is producing for us an eternal weight of glory far beyond all comparison" (2 Corinthians 4:17).

However, many people at that time will not know Jesus Christ as their Savior. Because of this, before the Lord's wrath of the Lamb judgments fall, God in His mercy will give every person on earth one last opportunity to come to faith in Jesus Christ and be saved by enabling the gospel to be preached to the whole world.

## Gospel Will Be Preached to the Whole World

During the great tribulation the persecution of the church will be so intense that "no one can work" (John 9:4); that is, in traditional mass communication of the gospel. But "with God all things are possible" (Mark 10:27 KJV). Jesus says the gospel will be preached to the whole world:

> This gospel of the kingdom will be preached in the whole world as a testimony to all nations, and then the end will come. (Matthew 24:14 NIV)

Every evangelistic crusade and camp meeting revival has a last altar call. When the gospel is preached to the whole world, this will be the last altar call for lost humanity.

How will God accomplish this worldwide proclamation of the gospel?

Revelation 14:6-7 describes an angel flying high in the air who had "an eternal gospel to preach to those who live on the earth, and to every nation and tribe and tongue and people." The angel has a message of repentance — telling lost humanity to fear God and give Him glory — before judgment (the wrath) falls.

Who is this angel?

In The Revelation angels represent literal angels or are figurative for Christian pastors, such as "the angel of the church in Smyrna" (v.2:8) believed to be Ante-Nicene father and bishop Polycarp (he was a student of apostle John) who in martyrdom was "faithful until death" (v.2:10). The *New Bible Commentary* remarks:

> A last warning is given to the unbelieving of humanity. All the nations are summoned to repentance and the worship of God. The message is called *the eternal gospel,* since the eternal blessings of the good news still remain for those

who will respond. Observe that the representation of an angel preaching the gospel is part of the symbolism of the prophecies; the term "angel" means messenger, and the messengers are of flesh and blood.[20]

*The Bible Reader's Companion* also comments about the final proclamation of the gospel of Jesus Christ: "Even on the eve of [wrath] judgment, lost humanity is invited to turn and worship the Lord. Judgment is sure. But so is grace."[21]

After the gospel is preached to the whole world, Jesus said, "Then the end will come" Matthew 24:14).

Then, Christ's return will indeed be imminent as all the signs that Scripture foretells will precede the return of Jesus Christ and the resurrection and rapture of the church will be fulfilled.

Then, the birth pains of false Christs; wars and rumors of wars; famines; great earthquakes; plagues; extreme weather; terrors; supernatural signs in the sun, moon, and stars; distress of nations; lawlessness; and the tribulation of persecution—all which warn of the coming of Christ—will soon end!

Then, the church of Jesus Christ will soon be caught away to meet the Lord in the air, and afterwards, will soon forget the anguish of the birth pains, as Jesus foretells with an analogy:

A woman giving birth to a child has pain because her time has come; but when her baby is born she **forgets the anguish** (Gk., *thlípsis*, **tribulation, anguish**) because of her joy that a child is born into the world. (John 16:21 NIV)

However, my Christian friend, you will never forget the great and glorious resurrection and rapture day when the sky will roll back like a scroll and the church will be taken away.

# 10

# THE SKY ROLLED BACK

*The sky rolled back like a scroll. (Revelation 6:14 NIrV)*

O ne of the most cherished hymns of the nineteenth century is *It is Well with My Soul* that has these lines:

> *But Lord, 'tis for Thee, for Thy coming we wait,*
> *The sky, not the grave, is our goal;*
> *Oh, trump of the angel! Oh, voice of the Lord!*
> *Blessed hope, blessed rest of my soul.*
> *And Lord, haste the day when my faith shall be sight,*
> *The clouds be* **rolled back as a scroll***;*
> *The trump shall resound, and the Lord shall descend,*
> *A song in the night, oh my soul!*

From this hymn we gain a glimpse into how premillennialists from the early church to the nineteenth century understood Scriptural teaching about our Lord's return to ingather the church which conflicts with today's popular teaching.

For centuries many premillennialists held that our Lord Jesus will return at Revelation 6:14 at the opening of the sixth seal of The Revelation when the sky and clouds will roll "back as a scroll" and "the trump shall resound, and the Lord shall descend" to catch away His church.

Early church premillennialists interpreted Scripture to teach that Jesus

Christ will return in two phases. Specifically, they taught that Christ will return *for* His church at Revelation 6:14 before the wrath of the Lamb judgments begin, and that Christ will return *with* His church at the end of the wrath of the Lamb judgments at Armageddon.

With a countdown to His coming, this chapter presents the first phase of Christ's return *for* His church. It also presents what happens back on earth? And, what happens up in the clouds?

## Countdown to His Coming

### Final Hours of the Tribulation of Persecution

Apostle John foretells what will happen in the final hours of the tribulation of persecution when the sixth seal is opened. He says there will be "a great earthquake," the sun will darken, and the moon will turn "blood red" (Revelation 6:12 NIV). Old Testament prophet Joel also foretold what will happen:

> It will come about after this that I will pour out My Spirit on all mankind; and your sons and daughters will prophesy, your old men will dream dreams, your young men will see visions. Even on the male and female servants I will pour out My Spirit in those days. I will display wonders in the sky and on the earth, blood, fire and columns of smoke. The **sun will be turned into darkness** and the **moon into blood** before the great and awesome **day of the Lord** comes. (Joel 2:28-31)

Let's analyze the "day of the Lord." This is an expression that signifies "a time in which God actively intervenes in history, primarily for judgment."[1] In the past when judgment fell on ancient Babylon, it was called the "day of the Lord" (Isaiah 13:6). The next "day of the Lord" will be when Christ returns *for* His church, which Paul writes about in these passages:

> So that his spirit may be saved in the **day of the Lord** Jesus. (1 Corinthians 5:5)

The church of God . . . awaiting eagerly the revelation of
our Lord Jesus Christ, who will also confirm you to the end,
blameless in the **day of our Lord** Jesus Christ. (1 Corinthians
1:2, 7, 8)

## Final Minutes of the Tribulation of Persecution

As events at the opening of the sixth seal unfold, "stars in the sky"
will fall to the earth (Revelation 6:13 NIV). This can be interpreted
both literally and figuratively.

Literally, with the darkening of the sun the "stars in the sky" will
be more visible and could be shooting stars (meteors).

Figuratively, "stars in the sky" in Revelation 6 can be metaphorical
as in Chapter one which portrays Jesus holding "seven stars" (v.16):
"The seven stars are the angels of the seven churches" (v.20); the angels
being symbolic of bishops, or pastors, of the seven churches. Similar
imagery is found in the Old Testament when Joseph said he had a
dream that "the sun and the moon and eleven stars were bowing down
to me" (Genesis 37:9). The stars represented Joseph's brothers who
became heads of the tribes of Israel. Thus, stars in The Revelation can
symbolize Christian ministers and other believers in Christ.

Therefore, in Revelation 6:13 the "stars in the sky" that fall to earth
could be actual shooting stars or they could be symbolic of the Lord's
people who fall to earth faithful until death "in the last furious onset
of the power of Antichrist,"[2] remarked Tertullian. Ante-Nicene father
Victorinus also interpreted stars in this verse figuratively: "The falling
of the stars are the faithful who are troubled for Christ's sake . . . by
persecution."[3]

Rest assured, believer, in the final minutes of the tribulation of
persecution while you feel the earth quivering from earthquake, while
you see the sun growing dim, while you see the moon turning blood
red, while you see shooting stars streak across the sky, and while you
see the Antichrist's forces pursuing you to take your life, you can have
peace knowing at that point that our Lord's return is truly imminent!
It will be a fearful and trying time, but during a similar tribulation
Cyprian encouraged his church quoting Isaiah:

> Strengthen the feeble hands, steady the knees that give way;
> say to those with fearful hearts, "Be strong, do not fear; your
> God will come, **he will come with vengeance**; with divine
> retribution **he will come to save you**." (Isaiah 35:3-4 NIV)

Indeed, as Isaiah foretells, our Lord will come. He will come "with vengeance" and will pour out His wrath of the Lamb judgments on the ungodly followers of Antichrist left behind. But He will save you, my Christian friend, from it by resurrection or rapture.

## Immediately After the Tribulation of Persecution

Jesus said, "Immediately *after* the tribulation of those days the sun will be darkened, and the moon will not give its light, and the stars will fall from the sky, and the powers of the heavens will be shaken" (Matthew 24:29).

Then the climax of the Christian's journey—the blessed hope of the church—will unfold! The sky will roll "back like a scroll" (Revelation 6:14 NIrV). Like a huge scroll unrolling, the clouds and sky will roll back!

## FIRST PHASE RETURN: CHRIST RETURNS *FOR* HIS CHURCH

"Then the sign of the Son of Man [Jesus] will appear in the sky" (Matthew 24:30).

Christ's coming will be "just as the lightning comes from the east and flashes even to the west, so will the coming of the Son of Man be" (Matthew 24:27).

Then stock traders in New York skyscrapers as well as people all over the world will see omnipresent Jesus "coming on the clouds of the sky with power and great glory" (Matthew 24:30). It will be as St. John foretold, "Every eye will see Him, even those who pierced Him" (Revelation 1:7). Our Lord's coming will be as the Psalmist sang:

> Let the sea roar and all it contains, the world and those who
> dwell in it. Let the rivers clap their hands, let the mountains

sing together for joy before the Lord, for **He is coming** to judge the earth. (Psalm 98:7-9)

Fishermen out on the ocean bringing in their catch will hear the Lord shout! As St. Paul prophesied, "For the Lord Himself will descend from heaven with a shout, with the voice of the archangel" (1 Thessalonians 4:16).

Outside on the playground school children will hear the blowing of a trumpet as Paul also foretold, "For the trumpet will sound" (1 Corinthians 15:52).

At sports arenas multitudes will turn their eyes upward and see the Lord attended by thousands upon thousands of holy angels who will fill the sky from one end to the other. As Jesus foretold, "He will send forth His angels with a great trumpet and they will gather together His elect [His church] from the four winds, from one end of the sky to the other" (Matthew 24:31).

Airline passengers will witness white-robed saints ascending to meet the Lord in the air. As St. Paul foretells: "The dead in Christ will rise first" (1 Thessalonians 4:16). "Behold, I tell you a mystery; we will not all sleep, but we will all be changed, in a moment, in the twinkling of an eye, at the last trumpet; for the trumpet will sound, and the dead will be raised imperishable, and we will be changed. For this perishable must put on the imperishable, and this mortal must put on immortality" (1 Corinthians 15:51-53). This is "the first resurrection" (Revelation 20:6); the resurrection of the righteous.

Those in chains persecuted for Christ's sake will hear the Lord shouting to them: "Come out, my people! Come out from her! You must not take part in her sins; you must not share in her punishment!" (Revelation 18:4 GNT). Here He pleads for the church to come out of Babylon, figurative for the world's last empire, the Antichrist's, and so avoid the wrath of the Lamb judgments about to befall Babylon.

Then faithful Christians all around the world will sense that it is time to meet the Lord in the air. As Paul said: "Then we who are alive and remain will be caught up [the rapture] together with them in the clouds to meet the Lord in the air" (1 Thessalonians 4:17). (Modern teaching of multiple raptures and multiple first resurrections are not

Scriptural). It will be as Jesus foretold:

> Two men will be in the field; one will be taken [in rapture]
> and the other left [behind]. Two women will be grind-
> ing with a hand mill; one will be taken and the other left.
> (Matthew 24:40-41 NIV)

The famed early church theologian and Ante-Nicene father, Tertullian, writes about the coming of the Lord and the rapture of the church:

> Now the privilege of this favour awaits those who shall
> at the coming of the Lord be found in the flesh, and who
> shall, owing to the oppressions of **the time of Antichrist**,
> deserve by an instantaneous death, which is accomplished
> by a sudden change, to become qualified to join the rising
> saints [**the rapture**]; as he writes to the Thessalonians: "For
> this we say unto you by the word of the Lord, that we which
> are alive and remain unto the coming of the Lord shall
> not prevent them which are asleep. For the Lord Himself
> shall descend from heaven with a shout, with the voice of
> the archangel, and with the trump of God: and the dead in
> Christ shall rise first: then we too shall ourselves be caught
> up together with them in the clouds, to meet the Lord in
> the air: and so shall we ever be with the Lord."[4]

At this point, the church will be with Jesus Christ in the sky.

## WHAT HAPPENS BACK ON EARTH?

Back on earth, the followers of Antichrist will recognize that they have been left behind. "Then all the tribes of the earth will mourn" (Matthew 24:30). These people who unjustly inflicted great tribulation of persecution on the church, to them, in the words of the legendary preacher of yesteryear, Dr. R.G. Lee, famed for his sermon *Payday Someday*, payday has come!

Our Lord Jesus Christ, the Almighty Lamb of God and the Judge of all mankind, in His justice and vengeance for His people, will repay the ungodly followers of Antichrist who persecuted His church, with the wrath of the Lamb judgments. The initial outpouring of the wrath of the Lamb is described by Apostle John:

> The great men and the commanders and the rich and the strong and every slave and free man hid themselves in the caves and among the rocks of the mountains; and they said to the mountains and to the rocks, "Fall on us and hide us from the presence of Him who sits on the throne, and from **the wrath of the Lamb**; for the great day of their wrath has come, and who is able to stand?" (Revelation 6:15-16)

## WHAT HAPPENS UP IN THE CLOUDS?

The blessed hope and glorious appearing of our great God and Savior Jesus Christ" (Titus 2:13 NKJV) will at that point become a reality for the church gathered with Christ up in the clouds.

Now, with creation having given birth to the children of God by resurrection and rapture at Christ's return, the sky that had rolled back as a scroll as the Lord descended from heaven to ingather His church, will now be rolled back up. As John the apostle relates:

> The sky receded like a scroll, rolling up [rolled away].
> (Revelation 6:14 NIV)

Early church Ante-Nicene father, theologian, and bishop Victorinus comments on Revelation 6:14:

> For the heaven [sky] to be rolled away, that is, that the **church shall be taken away**.[5]

As Victorinus here substantiates, this is the early church doctrine of the sixth seal post-"time, times and half a time" tribulation of persecution and pre-wrath of the Lamb judgments first phase return of Jesus Christ in the sky to resurrect and rapture the church. This great Scriptural truth and teaching about the timing of Christ's return and the rapture of the church was preached on three continents for the first three hundred years of the Christian faith and in pockets to the sixth century—it was lost in the dark ages but has now been rediscovered—and how simple, straightforward, and plain the Bible presents the fathers' early church premillennialism.

At this point the church will be welcomed into heaven.

After all this, the wrath of the Lamb judgments will be poured out on all the ungodly remaining on earth.

# 11

# WRATH OF THE LAMB

The love of God is without doubt the overarching theme of the New Testament. Indeed, "God is love" (1 John 4:8). Love emanates from His very Being. In all His dealings with us, even in His discipline, there is a consciousness of His love.

Amidst all our triumphs and trips, words fail when we attempt to grasp or perceive His love for us, particularly in that He sent His Son to provide salvation and eternal life for us. "For God so **loved** the world, that He gave His only begotten Son, that whoever believes in Him shall not **perish**, but have eternal life" (John 3:16).

In this familiar verse the word "loved" lifts our spirits. Another word in this verse, "perish," sorrows our souls. Why should anyone "perish?" The answer is the wrath of a holy and just God toward our sin and evil, as D.R.W. Wood writes in the *New Bible Dictionary*:

> The permanent attitude of the holy and just God when confronted by sin and evil is designated his "wrath." . . . It is . . . a personal quality, without which God would cease to be fully righteous and his love would degenerate into sentimentality. His wrath, however, even though like his love it has to be described in human language, is not wayward, fitful or spasmodic, as human anger always is. It is as permanent and as consistent an element in his nature as is his love.[1]

Yes, God is "abounding in love" (Numbers 14:18 NIV). But He is also just. And perfect justice demands that sin and evil be punished. This is why God is a God to be feared because His justice demands that He punish sin and evil (Ecclesiastes 12:13-14). Wrath executes divine justice. To grasp this subject, this chapter will discuss the Bearer of our justice and wrath, Jesus Christ; why God delays His justice; how should we respond to injustice?; the difference between tribulation and wrath; why the church will be removed before the wrath; and what transpires during the wrath of the Lamb?

## Bearer of Our Justice and Wrath, Jesus Christ

You and I once stood in the crosshairs—sinners before Holy God who justly deserved His wrath, death, and eternal separation from Him. "But God, being rich in mercy, because of His great love with which He loved us" (Ephesians 2:4) sent His Son, Jesus, to be our Savior. As a substitutionary sacrifice, Jesus Christ the Lamb of God, took upon Himself on the cross the justice and wrath that we deserved to pay and paid for our sins on our behalf: "The righteous for the unrighteous, that he might bring us to God" (1 Peter 3:18 ESV).

Because of what Christ did for you and me on the cross, there is no need for anyone to suffer the wrath of God. Forgiveness, salvation, and eternal life are available to every person who in repentance and faith will turn to Jesus Christ in prayer trusting Him as their Savior and Lord. As the Bible says, "Whoever believes in Him shall not perish, but have eternal life" (John 3:16).

However, many people choose not to follow Jesus Christ. Even though Jesus paid for their sins on the cross, many of them are trying to go to heaven another way besides through Christ. They hope their good deeds will outnumber their bad deeds and that this will get them into heaven. However, they do not consider that Holy God requires the same of us that He requires of Himself—absolute sinless perfection—which only Christ's imputed righteousness can provide.

There are other people who are openly hostile towards Jesus Christ and His people. They inflict violent unjust persecution upon the Christian community. In China, Africa, and the Middle East, Christians today face nothing short of biblical tribulation. Are they suffering the end of days tribulation of persecution that Jesus spoke about? At this writing, no!

Although the end of days tribulation will be one of the worst, there have been other tribulations in church history. Some of the most severe were the great persecution by the Jews (Acts 8:1), and those by Roman Emperors Nero, Domitian, and Diocletian.

Because tribulation has been inflicted upon the church in the past, and continues to this day, you can be assured, my Christian friend, that our Lord Jesus Christ, the Lamb of God who is just, will repay the ungodly of this world for unjustly persecuting His people. However, God is patient and often delays His justice.

## WHY GOD DELAYS HIS JUSTICE

Yes, many of those tribulations of the church happened long ago. If God was going to judge He would have done so by now, right? But in Scripture we find that God often delays His justice? He gives people time to repent.

Moreover, if God had judged the world immediately after the first great persecution by the Jews (Acts 8:1), who would have been swept away in His wrath? Would it not have been a young man, a feared persecutor of Christians, who turned to follow Jesus Christ and who became the great apostle Paul?

Yes, fortunately for us, "The Lord is slow to anger, abounding in love and forgiving sin and rebellion. Yet he does not leave the guilty unpunished" (Numbers 14:18 NIV). In other words, if there is no repentance, payday will come as it did to Ahab and Jezebel.

In ancient Israel, King Ahab ruled the northern kingdom within which was Naboth's picturesque vineyard. Ahab wanted to buy it from him. However, the vineyard had been in Naboth's family for generations and he was not willing to sell it. So Ahab's wife, Jezebel, plotted a wicked scheme to steal it from him. Even though Naboth was a righteous man, Jezebel arranged to have him falsely accused, and as a result, he was taken outside the city and stoned to death.

When Ahab heard what his wife had done, instead of rebuking her, he was happy. Immediately, he left to take possession of Naboth's vineyard, but when he arrived he encountered among the vines an unexpected visitor—Elijah, the prophet of God. Knowing the truth that Naboth had been falsely accused and murdered, Elijah told Ahab: "'Thus says the Lord, "In the place where the dogs licked up the blood of Naboth the dogs will lick up your blood, even yours."'... "Of Jezebel also has the Lord spoken saying, 'The dogs will eat Jezebel'" (1 Kings 21:19,23).

As the seasons for grape picking passed there is no record that dogs ever bothered Ahab. But after three years a man aiming at nothing shot an arrow and it struck Ahab in his chariot, wounding him fatally. When they were cleaning his chariot, "Dogs licked up his blood" (1 Kings 22:38). God's payday someday—His wrath judgment—had finally come.

More years would pass before God dealt with Jezebel. In about the thirteenth year after Jezebel's wicked scheme to falsely accuse and murder Naboth, Jezebel's officials threw her out of the palace window to her death. When they went to bury Jezebel they found that dogs had eaten her, devouring her flesh to the point where all that remained was her skull, her feet, and the palms of her hands (2 Kings 9:35). It happened just as the prophet Elijah had said, "The dogs will eat Jezebel" (1 Kings 21:23). God's payday someday—His wrath judgment—had finally come.

Yes, God gave even Ahab and Jezebel time to repent, but they did not. So, eventually, God's just payday for what they had done came upon them. However, there was a period of years when it appeared that they had gotten away with injustice. So, how should we respond when we are victims of injustice?

## How Should We Respond to Injustice?

Jesus was a victim of injustice. He was falsely accused of plotting to destroy the temple (Mark 14:58), of being a drunkard (Matthew

11:19), and of breaking the Sabbath (John 9:16). He wrongly suffered persecution. How does God's Word instruct us to respond when we are victims of injustice, such as suffering unjust persecution? The Bible tells us: "Never take your own revenge, beloved, but leave room for the wrath of God, for it is written, 'Vengeance is Mine, I will repay,' says the Lord" (Romans 12:19). In other words, when we are victims of injustice we are to forgive, to set the matter right legally if necessary, and to leave the matter with God.

Still, from a human standpoint we often expect God to avenge the injustice immediately. But God's ways are not our ways. Besides, God loves our enemies as much as He loves us. So He gives them time to repent, and if they do, this turns away God's wrath and brings His forgiveness.

In the third century during the Decian persecution, Cyprian's church faced severe tribulation. Yet, Ante-Nicene father and bishop Cyprian explained that when the church suffers unjustly that we are to wait on the Lord and on His day of future vengeance (the wrath of the Lamb) and not hurry to avenge our suffering:

> I know, beloved brethren, that very many are eager, either on account of the burden or the pain of smarting wrongs, to be quickly avenged of those who act harshly and rage against them, we must not withhold the fact in the furthest particular, that placed as we are in the midst of these storms of a jarring world, and, moreover, the **persecutions** ... [we are to] patiently **wait for the day of [Christ's] vengeance** and not hurry to revenge our suffering with a querulous haste, since it is written, "Wait ye upon me, saith the Lord, in the day of my rising up for a testimony; for my judgment is to the congregations of the nations ... and pour out upon them my fury [Zephaniah 3:8]." The Lord commands us to wait, and to bear with brave patience **the day of future vengeance** [the wrath of the Lamb]; and He also speaks in the Apocalypse, saying ... Behold, I come quickly; and my reward is with me, to render to every man according to his

deeds [Revelation 22:12]."Whence also the martyrs, crying out and hastening with grief breaking forth to their revenge, are bidden still to **wait,** and to give patience for the times to be fulfilled and the martyrs to be completed. "And when He had opened," says he, "the fifth seal, I saw under the altar of God the souls of them that were slain for the word of God, and for their testimony; and they cried with a loud voice, saying, How long, O Lord, holy and true, dost Thou not judge and avenge our blood on them that dwell on the earth? And there were given to them each white robes; and it was said unto them that they should rest yet for a little season. . . . Let us wait for Him, beloved brethren, our Judge and Avenger [Jesus], who [when He comes] shall equally **avenge with Himself the congregation of His church."**[2]

The Lord has not yet avenged the suffering of Cyprian's church. Neither has the Lord avenged the modern church who is suffering severe persecution in some parts of the world. And yet, this unjust persecution of the church will intensify until it brings the tribulation of persecution at the hands of the Antichrist whose followers will kill so many Christians that Babylon will be, so to speak, "drunk with the blood of the saints, and with the blood of the witnesses of Jesus" (Revelation 17:6).

Nevertheless, my Christian brother or sister, you can be assured that our Lord Jesus Christ, the Lamb of God who is just, will avenge His church for the injustice inflicted upon His people. It will be a dreadful time called in Scripture the wrath of the Lamb, not tribulation.

## THE DIFFERENCE BETWEEN TRIBULATION AND WRATH

When the influential Dr. Scofield deviated from nineteen centuries of Christian teaching that the duration of the tribulation period will be for "a time, times, and half a time" (Daniel 12:7) within the final seven years, and introduced his seven-year tribulation theory, dispensationalists began calling the entire seventieth week of Daniel, The Tribulation.

Thus, the final seven years comprised of the beginning of birth pains in the early years; the time, times, and half a time tribulation period in the middle years; and the wrath of the Lamb judgments in the latter months of the seventieth week are taught in pretribulational dispensational premillennialism, a widely held view today, to be tribulation. Dispensationalists assert that tribulation and wrath are the same.

However, the following biblical Greek study indicates that tribulation and wrath are different.

## Tribulation

*Thlípsis*, Gk., means to crush or to press together and is variously translated as **tribulation**, persecution, distress, suffering, hardship, trouble, anguish, and affliction. This Greek word mostly denotes hardships or tribulations often stemming from persecution inflicted upon Christ's followers by an ungodly world. Although dispensationalists agree with this interpretation of tribulation, they contend that the end of days Tribulation is different. But this assertion has no biblical basis. Apostle John was a "fellow partaker in the tribulation [persecution]" (Revelation 1:9). Paul reminds Christians that "we must through many tribulations enter the kingdom of God" (Acts 14:22 NKJV).

## Wrath

*Orgé*, Gk., means **wrath**, vengeance, anger, retribution, and revenge, and is predominantly translated as wrath. *Orgé* often denotes "divine punishment based on God's angry judgment toward someone ... there is an implication of God's anger because of evil."[3] The *Theological Dictionary of the New Testament* adds that "*orgé* is especially oriented to revenge or punishment. Thus it is applied to rulers who must avenge injustice."[4]

Therefore, it is evident from this biblical Greek word study that *thlípsis* (tribulation) and *orgé* (wrath) have vastly different meanings.

Further, the difference between tribulation and wrath is illustrated in the biblical story of Naboth, Ahab, and Jezebel. Righteous Naboth experienced tribulation when he suffered the injustice of a false accusation and was murdered. Years later, Ahab and Jezebel experienced the **wrath** of God, who is just, when He avenged the injustice and punished them for inflicting unjust tribulation on Naboth. God's wrath judgment was terrible — dogs ate Jezebel beyond recognition. God's payday someday finally came.

In the same way, God the Son, Jesus Christ the Lamb of God, will avenge the injustice inflicted on the church during the end of days **tribulation** of persecution by ungodly followers of Antichrist by punishing them with the **wrath** of the Lamb, the terrible judgments described in The Revelation beginning with the seventh seal (Revelation 8). His wrath judgment will be terrible. God's payday someday will have finally come.

Therefore, it is plainly evident that tribulation and wrath are not the same. Frankly, dispensationalists should know better.

So, why do dispensationalists interpret tribulation and wrath to be the same? It is because of how they interpret dispensations.

In dispensational eschatology, tribulation and wrath are non-issues. Why? Because dispensationalists teach that Israel and the church are distinct, and they believe that the church must absolutely be removed off the earth before Israel can begin her seventieth week, her final seven year dispensation. Amazingly, they teach this despite the fact that they have no Scriptural proof.

So, to dispensationalists, the events that occur during the final seven years are irrelevant because they believe they will be absent from whatever transpires. This is why dispensationalists so easily accepted the seven-year tribulation theory, which theorizes that every event during the final seven years is tribulation, even though the seventieth week contains three major different events. To them, the final seven years is another dispensation and they won't be here (so they think!).

However, there is one common position expressed by early church premillennialists, Ante-Nicene fathers, who wrote on the subject, and that is, that the church will endure the "time, times, and half a time" (Daniel 12:7) tribulation of persecution (in the middle part of the final seven years), but will be removed before the wrath of the Lamb judgments (in the latter part of the final seven years) at Christ's first phase return in the sky.

## THE CHURCH REMOVED BEFORE THE WRATH

The return of Christ is the hope of the church. But it is terror and doom for the ungodly who will do the bidding of the Antichrist and who will persecute the church with great tribulation. They will face Christ's wrath.

Yet, before our Lord's wrath falls, the Bible and early church premillennialists teach that Jesus Christ will remove the church. Ante-Nicene father Victorinus explains:

> For the **wrath** of God always strikes the obstinate people with seven plagues, that is, perfectly, as it is said in Leviticus; and these shall be in the last time, when the **church shall have gone out of the midst.**"[5]

When Jesus Christ returns coming on the clouds to resurrect and rapture His church to meet Him in the air, once His people are gathered to Him in the sky, there will be an initial outpouring of Christ's wrath upon the ungodly left behind on earth:

> Then all the tribes of the earth will mourn (Matthew 24:30). The rich and the strong and every slave and freeman, hid themselves in the caves and among the rocks of the mountains; and they said to the mountains and to the rocks, "Fall on us and hide us from the presence of Him who sits on the throne, and from **the wrath of the Lamb**; for the great day of their wrath has come, and who is able to stand?"(Revelation 6:16,17)

After this initial outpouring of Christ's wrath, Jesus will escort His bride, the church, to His heavenly home. Then the sky will roll "up like a scroll" (Revelation 6:14 NLT). As Victorinus declared, "That the church shall be taken away."[6]

Arriving at her Bridegroom's abode far away, Jesus will present her, the church, to the Father and will lavish upon her the finest at "the marriage supper of the Lamb" (Revelation 19:9).

Then, calm blankets the earth.

### Calm on Earth

After Jesus Christ removes the church to heaven, the earth becomes calm. Not even the wind blows (Revelation 7:1).

Sensing the strange quiet, people remaining will likely come walking out of caves and from behind boulders and trees and ask: "Is that it, is it over?" But the stillness from suspension in wrath judgments is only temporary until angels "put a seal on the foreheads of the servants of our God" (Revelation 7:3 NIV). St. John tells us who these servants are and how many:

> One hundred and forty-four thousand sealed from every tribe of the sons of Israel. From the tribe of Judah, twelve thousand were sealed, from the tribe of Reuben twelve thousand ... [and continuing, twelve thousand from each of the twelve tribes]. (Revelation 7:4-5)

These Israelites being sealed are of modern national Israel. These national Jews followed neither the Antichrist nor Jesus Christ, and so were not raptured. Counterparts to them in Old Testament times were Maccabean Jews who lived during the reign of Antiochus IV Epiphanes (a type of Antichrist). These followed the example of the Maccabean Jews who revolted against Antiochus' desecration of the temple and Jewish religious rites.

Much of the same will happen in the days of Antichrist. Initially, apostate national Israel will consider him their long-awaited messiah. But, when this counterfeit breaks his covenant with Israel and stops the temple sacrifices (Daniel 9:27), exposing his true nature, many religiously observant Jews will revolt against him, bringing great persecution on themselves from the Antichrist.

Yet, even though these devout Jews will be left behind because of unbelief. When they see Jesus "coming with the clouds, and every eye will see Him, even those who pierced Him" (Revelation 1:7), they will know that Jesus really is Israel's Messiah, and will turn in faith to Him, fulfilling Romans 11:23. As a result, the Lord will have mercy on them and will place a "seal" on them to protect them from the wrath judgments. (This is the only mention in Scripture of God's protection during the wrath). Utley comments about the seal:

> The purpose of the seal is to identify God's people so that the wrath of God will not affect them. Satan's [Antichrist's] seal identifies his people, who are the object of God's wrath. . . . Satan seals all of his followers, as does God (Revelation 22:4).[7]

Walvoord also explains:

> The seal on their foreheads symbolizes protection and ownership and God's intention to protect the twelve tribes that are mentioned.[8]

This number, twelve thousand, sealed from each of the twelve tribes of Israel, totaling one hundred and forty-four thousand, has been long debated. Scholars are divided as to whether this number is literal or symbolic. Yet, recognizing that The Revelation abounds in imagery and symbolism, and recognizing that the number "twelve" is symbolic in Scripture for "chosen" (e.g. chosen twelve apostles), and recognizing that the Greek word translated "thousand" is plural (*chiliades*, thousands), we can logically determine that the number is likely symbolic for the "chosen thousands" from each tribe with the total (12 x 12) being "all of the chosen thousands" of Israel. God knows the exact number. But many believers interpret the number as literally 144,000.

Concerning these newly believing 144,000 or "all of the chosen thousands" of Israel that will be saved during the wrath and sealed by God on their foreheads to protect them from the wrath judgments, *A Commentary, Critical and Explanatory, on the Old and New Testaments* explains that they "shall form the nucleus on earth of the Israelite nation that is from this time to stand at the head of the millennial nations of the world."[9]

Although calm has reigned over the earth while these newly believing Israelite Christians are being sealed, it is quite the opposite in heaven.

## Loud Rejoicing in Heaven

By contrast, the church in heaven will be rejoicing loudly, as John the apostle relates:

> A great multitude that no one could count, from every nation, tribe, people and language, standing before the throne and in front of the Lamb. They were wearing white robes and were holding palm branches in their hands. And they cried out in a **loud voice**: "Salvation belongs to our God, who sits on the throne, and to the Lamb." (Revelation 7:9-10 NIV)

But between the loud praises one of the elders asks John:

> "These who are clothed in the white robes, who are they, and from where have they come?" And I [John] said to him, "My lord, you know." And he said to me, "These are the ones who come out of the **great tribulation** [of persecution], and they have washed their robes and made them white in the blood of the Lamb. For this reason, they are before the throne of God ... and He who sits on the throne will spread His tabernacle over them. They will hunger no longer, nor thirst anymore; nor will the sun beat down on them, nor any heat; for the Lamb in the center of the throne will be their shepherd, and will guide them to springs of the water of life; and God will wipe every tear from their eyes." (Revelation 7:13-17)

But, then, abruptly, the loud rejoicing stops. Heaven is silent (Revelation 8:1).

## Heaven is Silent

"When the Lamb broke the seventh seal, there was silence in heaven" (Revelation 8:1).

Why? Because, you see, the day holds a paradox.

Yes, it is a day of rejoicing for the church, the bride of Christ. But it is also a day and a time now to be silent and sad because judgment is about to be poured out over the ungodly on earth who committed sinful, murderous, and evil acts against Christ's church.

And "there was silence in heaven for about half an hour" (Revelation 8:1).

## A Parallel

Here, an interesting parallel can be drawn between the Noahic Floodwaters of wrath in Genesis and the wrath of the Lamb judgments in The Revelation. Jesus said, "Just as it happened in the days of Noah, so it shall be also in the days of the Son of Man" (Luke 17:26).

It is common knowledge that during the Noahic Flood it rained "for forty days and forty nights" (Genesis 7:12). But a lesser known fact is that the Floodwaters "prevailed upon the earth one hundred and fifty days [**five months**]" (Genesis 7:24). A similar timeframe is given during the wrath of the Lamb — "**five months**" (Revelation 9:5,10).

Thus, the Noahic Flood of God's wrath poured out on the ungodly left behind while God's people in the ark — rose up above the highest mountains to where the clouds drift — is a parallel. This is a type of the wrath of the Lamb that will be poured out on the ungodly left behind while God's people — rise up to the drifting clouds — to meet Jesus in the air and onward to heaven. Scripture also gives the same timeframe for both, **five months** (Genesis 7:24; Revelation 9:5,10).

## Teaching about the Church and the Wrath of the Lamb

Although there will be an initial outpouring of Christ's wrath at His sixth seal return to ingather the church by resurrection and rapture, it is at the opening of the seventh seal in Revelation 8 that the judgments of the wrath of the Lamb begin.

This said, our amillennialist and historic premillennialist friends teach that the church will be left on earth, but protected during the terrible wrath of the Lamb judgments. Blomberg and Chung in *A Case for Historic Premillennialism* remark:

Believers—God's servants on earth protected from his wrath during the outpouring of the twenty-one judgments.[10]

However, Paul the apostle explains why the church will **not** be left on earth during the terrible wrath of the Lamb judgments, but will instead be rescued from the wrath by Jesus when He returns from heaven. As Paul declares:

Wait for His Son from heaven, whom He raised from the dead, that is Jesus, who **rescues us** from the wrath to come. (1 Thessalonians 1:10)

In other words, Jesus will rescue His church (remove the church off the earth by resurrection and rapture) **before** the terrible wrath of the Lamb judgments begin. Moreover, Scripture tells followers of Jesus Christ that "God has not destined us for wrath, but for obtaining salvation through our Lord Jesus Christ" (1 Thessalonians 5:9).

However, one argument for the church remaining on earth, but protected, during the wrath is because ancient Israel was protected from a type of the wrath judgments that were poured out on Egypt before the Exodus (Chs. 7-11). As discussed, the unbelieving 144,000 or "all of the chosen thousands" of modern national Israel—who will be left on earth because of unbelief at Christ's first phase return and the rapture but who will come to saving faith in Jesus Christ during the months of wrath—they, like ancient Israel, will be left on earth, but protected, during the wrath of the Lamb judgments.

As for the church on earth at the time of Christ's first phase return, the sequence of events in the Book of Revelation places the church in heaven *before* the wrath judgments begin, with the following progressive steps:

**Step One—Revelation 6:14**: When the sky rolls back the church is taken away by resurrection and rapture at Christ's first phase sixth seal return.

**Step Two—Revelation 7:14**: The resurrected and raptured church that came "out of the great tribulation" is with Jesus in heaven "standing before the throne and before the Lamb," Jesus Christ (v. 7:9).

**Step Three — Revelation 8**: The <u>first</u> wrath judgment begins on earth with the opening of the seventh seal.

Although not all events in The Revelation are sequential, the progressive steps in Revelation 6-8 indicate chronological order, with the resurrected and raptured church in heaven **before** the first wrath judgment.

With the church safe in heaven, the Lamb of God, Jesus Christ, will break the seventh seal and the judgments of the wrath of the Lamb will now be justly poured out on the ungodly followers of Antichrist left behind on earth who unjustly persecuted His church with tribulation.

## WHAT TRANSPIRES DURING THE WRATH OF THE LAMB?

With the opening of the seventh seal in Revelation 8, the wrath of the Lamb judgments begin. Pictured are seven angels holding seven trumpets. As each of the seven angels sound their trumpet, calamitous judgments, woes, and bowls of wrath ensue:

### Trumpet Judgments

**First Trumpet**: The first angel sounded his trumpet "and there came hail and fire, mixed with blood, and they were thrown to the earth; and a third of the earth was burned up, and a third of the trees were burned up, and all the green grass was burned up" (Revelation 8:7).

**Second Trumpet**: The second angel sounded his trumpet "and something like a great mountain burning with fire was thrown into the sea; and a third of the sea became blood . . . and a third of the ships were destroyed" (Revelation 8:8, 9).

**Third Trumpet**: The third angel sounded his trumpet "and a great star fell from heaven, burning like a torch, and it fell on a third of the rivers and on the springs of waters" (Revelation 8:10).

**Fourth Trumpet**: The fourth angel sounded "and a third of the sun, and a third of the moon and a third of the stars were smitten, so that a third of them might be darkened and the day might not shine for a third of it" (Revelation 8:8,9).

## First Woe

**Fifth Trumpet**: The fifth angel sounded his trumpet and the bottom-less pit [the abyss] was opened "and smoke went up out of the pit, like the smoke of a great furnace; and the sun and the air were darkened by the smoke of the pit. And out of the pit came forth locusts upon the earth; and power was given them, as the scorpions of the earth have power. . . . And they were not permitted to kill anyone, but to torment for **five months**; and their torment was like the torment of a scorpion when it stings a man.

And in those days men will seek death and will not find it; they will long to die, and death flees from them. And the appearance of the locusts was like horses prepared for battle . . . and they have tails like scorpions, and stings; and in their tails is their power to hurt men for **five months**" (Revelation 9:2,3,5-7,10).

## Second Woe

**Sixth Trumpet**: The sixth angel sounded his trumpet and "four angels who are bound at the great river Euphrates . . . were released, so that they might kill a third of mankind" (Revelation 9:13,15).

## Third Woe

Given to the seven angels were "seven golden bowls full of the wrath of God" (Revelation 15:7).

## Bowl Judgments

**Judgment One**: The first angel "poured out his bowl into the earth; and it became a loathsome and malignant sore upon the men who had the mark of the beast [the Antichrist] and who worshipped his image" (Revelation 16:2).

**Judgment Two**: The second angel "poured out his bowl into the sea, and it became blood . . . and every living thing in the sea died" (Revelation 16:3).

**Judgment Three**: The third angel "'poured out his bowl on the rivers and springs of water, and they became blood. Then I heard the angel in charge of the waters say: "You are just in these judgments, you who are and who were, the Holy One, because you have so judged; for they have shed the blood of your saints and prophets, and you have given them blood to drink as they deserve"' (Revelation 16: 4-6 NIV).

**Judgment Four**: The fourth angel "poured out his bowl upon the sun; and it was given to it to scorch men with fire" (Revelation 16:8).

**Judgment Five**: The fifth angel "poured out his bowl upon the throne of the beast [the Antichrist]; and his kingdom became darkened; and they gnawed their tongues because of pain, and they blasphemed the God of heaven because of their pains and their sores; and they did not repent of their deeds" (Revelation 16:10,11).

**Judgment Six**: The sixth angel "poured out his bowl upon the great river Euphrates, and its water was dried up, to prepare the way for the kings from the east. . . . And they assembled them at the place that in Hebrew is called Armageddon" (Revelation 16:12,16 ESV).

**Judgment Seven**: The seventh angel "'poured out his bowl . . . and there was a great earthquake, such as there had not been since man came to be upon the earth. . . . And huge hailstones, about one hundred pounds each, came down from heaven upon men; and men blasphemed God because of the plague of the hail" (Revelation 16:17,18,21).

## Trumpet Judgments, Continued

**Seventh Trumpet**: "In the days of the . . . seventh angel, when he is about to sound, then the mystery of God is **finished**" (Revelation 10:7). And the seventh angel sounded his trumpet "and there arose loud voices in heaven, saying, The kingdom of the world has become the kingdom of our Lord, and of His Christ; and He will reign forever and ever" (Revelation 11:15).

### The Church in Heaven Praises God

St. John said, "After these things I heard what sounded like the loud voice of a vast throng in heaven, saying, "Hallelujah! Salvation and glory and power belong to our God, because his judgments are true and just. For he has judged . . . and has **avenged** the blood of his servants!" (Revelation 19:1-2 NET).

### Wrath Judgments Will Be Terrible

These wrath of the Lamb judgments will be terrible, but so were the deeds terrible that were committed by the ungodly in the days of Nero, Domitian, and Diocletian who fed our Christian forebears to lions, murdered them on racks, tore them apart by wild horses, and according to *Foxe's Book of Martyrs*, exhausted invention "to devise tortures against such as had no crime."[11]

Yes, these wrath judgments will be terrible, but so are the deeds terrible that are being committed in our times by the ungodly in the Middle East, China, and Africa in their unjustly imprisoning and murdering Christians.

Yes, these wrath judgments will be terrible, but so will the deeds be terrible that will be committed by the Antichrist and his followers during "the tribulation of the persecution which is to fall upon the church from the adversary [the Antichrist]."[12] Indeed, our Lord Jesus

Christ, the Lamb of God, who is just and the Judge of all mankind, He will justly avenge the blood of His servants with His terrible wrath of the Lamb judgments (Revelation 19:2).

## Jerusalem Under Attack

At the end of the wrath, Jerusalem will come under attack by the Antichrist. Launching his assault from the hills of Armageddon, the Antichrist's armies will march on Jerusalem in all-out war against our Messianic Christian brethren—the 144,000 or "all of the chosen thousands" of modern national Israel. They will entreat the Lord for help, and will beckon us to come near:

> *While reposing in our Savior's home faraway we hear,*
> *National Israel beckoning us, will you come near?*
> *To them, once our Savior's enemies, but now so dear,*
> *We prepare to fly to their aid to hear them all cheer!*
>
> *– Robert Franklin*

So, on that day, mount up, my Christian friend. It will be time for the church to return from heaven to earth with Jesus Christ, the King of kings and Lord of lords, the Almighty God and our Savior, for the battle and the blaze at Armageddon.

# 12

# ARMAGEDDON

*Encamped along the hills of light,*
*Ye Christian soldiers, rise,*
*And press the battle ere the night*
*Shall veil the glowing skies.*
*Against the foe in vales below*
*Let all our strength be hurled;*
*Faith is the victory, we know,*
*That overcomes the world. . . .*

*Then onward from the hills of light,*
*Our hearts with love aflame,*
*We'll vanquish all the hosts of night,*
*In Jesus' conqu'ring name.*

— *Faith is the Victory*, by John H. Yates *(1891)*

After reposing with our Bridegroom in His heavenly home of light, the church returns with King Jesus to battle the Beast and his armies in the great conflict between good and evil—the Battle of Armageddon!

You may ask: What causes the Battle of Armageddon? What will be accomplished at Armageddon? And, what changes to earth's topography will happen at Armageddon?

## WHAT CAUSES THE BATTLE OF ARMAGEDDON?

During the wrath of the Lamb, the 144,000 or "all of the chosen thousands" of national Israel will come to faith in Jesus Christ as their Messiah. This will spark the anger of Christ's enemy, the Antichrist. Consequently, the Antichrist will gather his armies from "all the nations" (Zechariah 12:3) to attack these Messianic Jews at Jerusalem, prompting their cry to the Lord for help and persuading King Jesus to return with the church from heaven to earth to fight for Israel. St. John declares:

> I saw heaven opened, and behold, a white horse, and He who sat on it is called Faithful and True, and in righteousness He judges and wages war. His eyes are a flame of fire. . . . And the armies which are in heaven . . . were following Him on white horses (Revelation 19:11,12,14).

When the true King of the Jews, Jesus Christ, sets foot back on earth, "on the Mount of Olives, which is in front of Jerusalem on the east" (Zechariah 14:4), the 144,000 or "all of the chosen thousands" of modern national Israel will cheer, and weep with tears of joy over Him like a long lost son returning home. Old Testament prophet Zechariah foretells:

> They will look on Me [Jesus] whom they have pierced; and they will mourn for Him, as one mourns for an only son, and they will weep bitterly over Him like the bitter weeping over a firstborn. . . . And one will say to him, "What are these wounds between your arms?" Then He will say, "Those with which I was wounded in the house of my friends." (vss. 12:10;13:6)

Then Jesus will go forth to fight for Israel, destroying all the nations that have come against Jerusalem in the great Battle of Armageddon:

In that day I [Jesus] will set about to **destroy all the nations** that come against Jerusalem. . . . For I will gather all the nations against Jerusalem to battle [Armageddon]. . . . Then the Lord will go forth and fight against those nations, as when He fights on a day of battle. (Zechariah 12:9; 14:2,3)

The Antichrist and his armies from all nations will expect to destroy the Lord's people at Jerusalem but their wicked plans will be foiled. Instead, they will be the ones defeated when Almighty King Jesus returns with His heavenly army of saints to fight for Israel—this is what causes the Battle of Armageddon—in the great clash between good and evil, Armageddon.

Yet, Jesus will accomplish far more than victory over evil at Armageddon.

## WHAT WILL BE ACCOMPLISHED AT ARMAGEDDON?

The box office thriller *Armageddon*, about a massive asteroid on a collision course with earth, was the highest-grossing movie in 1998 worldwide.[1] In 1983, *The Day After*, a nuclear Armageddon film, was seen by over 100 million people.[2] Of course, not much was accomplished in these fictional Armageddon films except explosions and mayhem. But at the real Armageddon our Lord will right wrongs and will establish His millennial kingdom on earth.

Specifically, King Jesus will accomplish what remains unfulfilled of Daniel's seventy weeks prophecy. That is, "to finish the transgression, to make an end of sin, and to bring in everlasting righteousness" (Daniel 9:24). He will accomplish these things by:

### Throwing the Antichrist and False Prophet into Lake of Fire

John foretold that "the beast was seized, and with him the false prophet who performed the signs in his presence, by which he had deceived those who had received the mark of the beast and those who worshipped his image; these two were thrown alive into the lake of fire" (Revelation 19:20).

### Throwing Satan into the Abyss for a Thousand Years

As the apostle wrote, "And he [an angel] laid hold of the dragon, the serpent of old, who is the devil and Satan, and bound him for a thousand years, and threw him into the abyss, and shut it and sealed it over him, so that he should not deceive the nations any longer, until the thousand years were completed; after these things he must be released for a short time" (Revelation 20:2,3).

### Making the Land Desolate and Destroying the Sinners

At Armageddon the ungodly will:

> Wail, for the day of the Lord is near; it will come like destruction from the Almighty. Because of this, all hands will go limp, every man's heart will melt. Terror will seize them, pain and anguish will grip them; they will writhe like a woman in labor. They will look aghast at each other, their **faces aflame**. See, the day of the Lord is coming—a cruel day, with wrath and fierce anger—to **make the land desolate and destroy the sinners** within it. (Isaiah 13:6-9)

In Noah's day the floodwaters of God's wrath made the land desolate and destroyed the sinners within it (Genesis 7:21). Likewise, at Armageddon, King Jesus will "make the land desolate and destroy the sinners within it" (Isaiah 13:9), but this time with fire:

> **Fire** goes before Him [Jesus] and burns up His adversaries round about. His lightnings lit up the world; the earth saw and trembled. The mountains melted like wax at the presence of the Lord, at the presence of the Lord of the whole earth. (Psalm 97:3-5)

Old Testament prophet Malachi also foretells:

> "Surely the day is coming; it will burn like a furnace. All the arrogant and every evildoer will be stubble, and that day that

is coming will set them on **fire**," says the Lord Almighty. "Not a root or a branch will be left to them. But for you who revere my name [Christ's saints], the sun of righteousness will rise with healing in its wings. And you will go out and leap like calves released from the stall. Then you will trample down the wicked; **they will be ashes under the soles of your feet** on the day when I do these things," says the Lord Almighty. (Malachi 4:1-5 NIV)

Some believers interpret the fire at Armageddon as destroying (annihilating) the earth. But Malachi tells Christ's saints: "The wicked; they will be ashes under the soles of your feet." For there to be ashes under our feet it requires an earth remaining to stand on with ashes on its surface. Ante-Nicene father Minucius Felix comments on Malachi's prophecy:

In the flame of **fire** the Lord will judge the wicked. But the fire shall not touch the just. . . . Such will be the heat that the stones themselves shall melt. The winds assemble into lightnings, the heavenly wrath rages; and wherever the wicked man fleeth, he is seized upon by this fire. . . . Then after a thousand years [after the millennium] they are delivered over to Gehenna [the lake of fire].[3]

### Removing the Ungodly Dead into the Abyss for a Thousand Years

St. John writes of Armageddon and about all of the ungodly left behind on earth:

"The rest were killed with the sword which came from the mouth of Him [Jesus] who sat upon the horse, and all the birds were filled with their flesh. . . . The rest of the [ungodly] dead did not come to life until the thousand years were completed" (Revelation 19:21; 20:5).

### Protecting Believing Jews from Armageddon Fire

Omnipotent King Jesus will protect the 144,000 or "all of the chosen thousands" of modern national Israel:

> When you walk through the fire, **you will not be scorched**, nor will the flame burn you. For I am the Lord your God, the Holy One of Israel, your Savior. (Isaiah 43:2-3)

Just as the Lord protected the three Hebrews, Shadrach, Meshach, and Abednego, from blazing fire during the reign of Nebuchadnezzar (Daniel 3:26), so will King Jesus protect the new believers of modern national Israel from the blazing fire at Armageddon. Premillennialists hold that these surviving Jews will populate the earth during the millennium, when Jesus will refine their spiritual maturity, as Zechariah foretells:

> And I will bring **the third part through the fire**, refine them as silver is refined, and test them as gold is tested. They will call on My name, and I will answer them; I will say, "They are My people," And they will say, "The Lord is my God." (v. 13:9)

In contrast to modern times, Jews of modern national Israel will love and serve Jesus Christ as their Lord.

### Saving All Israel

At Armageddon all of Christ's holy people will be present. This includes spiritual Israel, which comprises Gentile believers grafted into the olive tree, Israel, and new believers from modern national Israel who will "be grafted back into their own olive tree" (Romans 11:24) forming the whole company of the redeemed of all the ages, the saints, the church of Jesus Christ. "Thus all Israel will be saved" (Romans 11:26), "the Israel of God" (Galatians 6:16).

Then, with Armageddon ended, and with only Christ and His people remaining on earth, King Jesus will remove the curse.

## Removing the Curse

The Fall of man into sin brought the curse, causing the earth to produce thorns and thistles and the atmosphere to produce tornadoes, floods, famines, and devastating hurricanes. But with sin removed from earth and righteousness beginning, our Holy Lord will remove the curse.

Zechariah foretells, "There will no longer be a curse" (v. 14:11). With the curse removed the fields will produce bountifully during Christ's millennial reign.

With King Jesus having accomplished these seven things at Armageddon, He can now prepare the earth and the sky for His visible earthly millennial reign with His saints. First, King Jesus transforms earth's topography.

### CHANGES TO EARTH'S TOPOGRAPHY AT ARMAGEDDON

Zechariah foretells about the renewing of earth's topography at Armageddon:

> In that day His [Christ's] feet will stand on the Mount of Olives . . . . All the **land will be changed into a plain** from Geba [Hebrew, "a hill."] to Rimmon south of Jerusalem; but **Jerusalem will rise** and remain on its site from Benjamin's Gate as far as the place of the First Gate to the Corner Gate, and from the Tower of Hananel to the king's wine presses. (vss. 14:4,10).

In addition to Jerusalem rising in elevation, King Jesus will answer centuries of prayers for "the peace of Jerusalem" (Psalm 122:6), about which Zechariah prophesies: "People will live in it . . . for Jerusalem will dwell in security" (v. 14:11).

With Jesus having accomplished at Armageddon what remained unfulfilled of Daniel's seventy weeks prophecy and having made improvements to earth's topography, next He will purify and renew the earth's surface and the sky for His millennial reign with His church.

However, many Christians today believe that the earth and sky will be burned up and destroyed (annihilation of the universe) at Armageddon, and that there will not be a subsequent millennium.

So, which is it? Earth and sky renewed **or** the universe burned up and destroyed?

# 13

# RENEWED OR DESTROYED?

Peter the apostle describes what will happen on the day of the Lord at Armageddon:

> The day of the Lord will come like a thief, in which the **heavens** will pass away with a roar and the **elements** will be **destroyed** with intense heat, and the earth and its works will be **burned up**. Since all these things are to be destroyed in this way, what sort of people ought you to be in holy conduct and godliness, looking for and hastening the coming of the day of God, because of which the heavens will be destroyed by burning, and the elements will melt with intense heat! (2 Peter 3:10-12)

Let's examine three interpretations of this passage. First, amillennialists, believe that we are presently living in the prophesied millennium and that there will not be a subsequent millennium. They, interpret 2 Peter 3:10-12 to teach that the earth and the heavens will be burned up and destroyed (annihilation of the universe) at Armageddon. However, this interpretation has problems, both scientifically and biblically.

Next, dispensational premillennialists contend that this passage does not refer to Armageddon, but rather to the post-millennium, at which time they teach that the universe will be burned up and destroyed. Yet, this interpretation also has problems: 1) Second Peter

3:12 speaks of "the day of the Lord" and "the day of God;" terms associated with Armageddon (Revelation 16:14). And, 2) Second Peter 3:12 describes this day as coming unexpectedly "like a thief" (2 Peter 3:10), language associated with Armageddon and not found in the post-millennium account of Revelation 20:7-10. Consequently, the dispensational premillennial interpretation of 2 Peter 3:10-12 also has problems scientifically and biblically.

Finally, early church premillennialists, like amillennialists, held that 2 Peter 3:10-12 refers to Armageddon. However, they did not interpret this passage to imply annihilation of the universe by fire at Armageddon, but rather held that this passage teaches that the earth and sky will be purified and renewed by fire at Armageddon in preparation for Christ's earthly, visible thousand year (millennial) reign with His church.

Asserting this third interpretation, Ante-Nicene father Methodius is emphatic that the burning of the earth and the sky at Armageddon is **not** for the purpose of destroying them (annihilation), but rather for "the purpose of purification and renewal:"[1]

> It is not satisfactory to say that the universe will be utterly destroyed, and sea and air and sky will be no longer. For the whole world will be deluged with fire from heaven, and **burnt for the purpose of purification and renewal**; it will not, however, come to complete ruin and corruption. . . . Wherefore the earth and the heaven must exist again [for the millennium] after the conflagration and shaking of all things.[2]

Yet, a simple reading of most translations of 2 Peter 3:10-12 suggests that the earth and the heavens will be burned up and destroyed (annihilation of the universe) at Armageddon, as amillennialists teach. However, it should be noted that translation from New Testament Greek to English can be influenced by a translator's eschatological view. For this reason, it is expedient that a New Testament Greek word study, a proposed more literal translation, and an exegesis be performed of 2 Peter 3:10-12. Also discussed is the dawn of the millennium.

## NT GREEK WORD STUDY OF 2 PETER 3:10-12

When scholars translate from biblical Greek (*koine* or "common" Greek in which the New Testament was written) to English, often three or four English words will accurately render a New Testament Greek word. Determining the equivalent word to use is based on context; both the immediate and greater context of Scripture. Scholars also recognize that a predisposition to a particular doctrinal or eschatological view can influence a translator's selection of an equivalent English word.

Therefore, it should be noted that amillennialism, which teaches no future millennium, and holds that the earth and the heavens will be destroyed (annihilation of the universe) by fire at Armageddon, has been the dominant eschatological view since the fifth century. Thus, it is possible over the centuries that this perspective has had some influence in the translation of 2 Peter 3:10-12.

Recognizing this possibility, three key New Testament Greek words from 2 Peter 3:10-12 and one emendation require some analysis here.

### "Heavens"

The Greek root word *ouranos* means heaven, sky, air and is translated "heavens" in 2 Peter 3:10, 12. Renderings of this Greek word are: "air" (Matthew 6:26 NASB); "sky" (Luke 4:25 HCSB); "heaven" (Luke 4:25 NKJV); and "heavens" (Luke 4:25 ESV).

In Genesis the atmosphere directly above the earth is referred to as the expanse and is called "**heaven**." "God made the expanse, and separated the waters which were below the expanse from the waters which were above the expanse; and it was so. God called the expanse heaven" (vss. 1:7-8). Thus, earth's atmosphere is called the **first heaven**.

A "Jewish concept, originally found in the Septuagint [is] that heaven is comprised of several spheres with God dwelling in the highest heaven."[3] Apostle Paul substantiates this: "I know a man in Christ who fourteen years ago . . . was caught up to the **third heaven**" (2 Corinthians 12:2). Among Jewish rabbis, "there were, according to a rabbinical theory, seven heavens, the seventh containing the throne of the Eternal."[4]

Although *ouranos* is generally rendered "heavens," *The Complete Word Study Dictionary: New Testament* explains that it can be translated "heaven" or "heavens": "The singular and plural are used similarly and interchangeably. There is no difference in meaning between them."[5]

Therefore, in 2 Peter 3:10,12, "heavens" is an accurate translation of *ouranos* but it can be misleading as only one sphere of heaven may be in view, and not the totality of the heavens. The *Greek-English Lexicon of the New Testament* comments that the referents to *ouranos* in 2 Peter 3:10,12 are **not** to multiple heavens as if including God's dwelling, but rather "the referents in this passage are the **sky** and the earth . . . but not the dwelling place of God."[6] Robertson also remarks: "In English we use "the heavens" usually for the canopy of **sky** above us."[7]

Thus, in 2 Peter 3:10-12 the proposed best English translation for *ouranos* is **lower heavens**. Specifically, the first heaven, or atmosphere, that was corrupted as a result of the Fall and the sky immediately beyond that has been corrupted by human activities.

### "Elements" and "Heavenly Bodies"

The Greek word in 2 Peter 3:10 & 12 is *stoicheia* which means "rudimentary elements . . . elementary doctrines . . . [and] in relation to the natural world (basic) elements, natural substances."[8] Renderings of this Greek word are: "elementary principles" (Hebrews 5:12 NASB); "elemental things" (Galatians 4:3 NASB); and "elements" (2 Peter 3:10 NASB). A number of respectable Bible versions translate *stoicheia* in 2 Peter 3:10-12 as "elements."

However, some translations render *stoicheia* in 2 Peter 3:10-12 as "heavenly bodies" (ESV & GNT), or "celestial bodies" (NET), or "galaxies" (The Message), but these renderings depart from the basic meaning.

Thus, the author agrees with Bible versions that translate *stoicheia* in 2 Peter 3:10-12 as "elements."

## "Destroyed" or "Dissolved"

The Greek word in 2 Peter 3:10-12 is a derivative of *luo*, meaning will be set free, released, loosed, and broke down. Renderings are: [set] "free" (1 Corinthians 7:27 RSV); "released" (1 Corinthians 7:27 NASB); "loosed" (1 Corinthians 7:27 NKJV); and "broke down" (Ephesians 2:14 NASB). By implication, "broke down" has been rendered in 2 Peter 3:10-12 as "destroyed" (NASB) and "dissolved" (ESV), yet the basic meaning of this word is to *set free*, *release*, or *loose* something. The *Analytical Lexicon of the Greek New Testament* comments:

> *luo* ... from a basic meaning "loose," translated with a variety of meanings from the specific contexts; (1) Literally, as freeing someone or something tied or bound "loose, untie, set free, release," figuratively, as freeing from a legal obligation "free, release "as freeing from spiritual bondage *set free* ... (2) Literally, as breaking something up into its component parts.[9]

Although translators of 2 Peter 3:10-12 have used the words "destroyed" or "dissolved" considered implied by *luo*, there are other Greek words for these that Peter uses in this same letter that he does not use in this passage. These are: "The world at that time was destroyed (Gk., *apollymai*; destroy, ruin) being flooded with water" (v. 3:6). And, "Will in the destruction (Gk., *phthora*; dissolved, destruction) of those creatures" (v. 2:12).

Although Peter could have used (*apollymai*; destroyed) or (*phthora*; dissolved, destruction) in 2 Peter 3:10-12, he chose instead to use a derivative of *luo* that basically means to *loose, release,* or *set free* something.

The question is: In 2 Peter 3:10-12 what are being **set free**? Answer: **Elements** — those on the earth's surface and in the sky.

Thus, literal translations proposed for verses 10 and 12 are:

> "*Elements* being burned will be *set free*" (2 Peter 3:10). And,

"[Lower] heavens [or, sky] being on fire will be *set free*, and the *elements* being burned with intense heat will melt" (2 Peter 3:12).

Since "elements being burned will be set free," it is important to have a scientific understanding of elements:

> The enormous variety of **matter** around you is made from different combinations of substances called **elements**. Elements are pure substances that cannot be broken down into anything simpler.[10]

An interesting fact about matter and elements was proven in 1694 by Antoine Lavoisier, the father of modern chemistry. Experimenting with a diamond enclosed in a glass jar, he and those assisting him used a large magnifying glass and focused a beam of the sun's hot rays on the diamond "and saw the diamond burn and disappear."[11]

Afterwards, although the diamond had burned and disappeared, "Lavoisier noted the overall **weight of the jar was unchanged** and that when it burned, the diamond had combined with oxygen to form carbon dioxide."[12] Lavoisier's experiment proved that **matter cannot be destroyed by burning**—nor can the universe.

Reason being, as Stewart notes in *Carbon Element Facts*, when matter burns its elements are released (set free) after which some combine with other elements and some change into carbon (i.e. soot or ashes) but the **matter still exists and has the same weight** although it exists in "different forms of the same element[s]."[13]

Therefore, Bible translations of 2 Peter 3:10-12 that render the derivative of *luo* as "destroyed" or "dissolved" are forcing an interpretation on the text and making a conclusion that is scientifically inaccurate.

This raises the question: How is the universe destroyed so new heavens and a new earth can be created? The Bible explains (discussed in Chapter 17).

Consequently, since it is scientifically proven that the universe (matter) cannot be destroyed by burning, 2 Peter 3:10-12 is clearly not about annihilation of the universe. Instead, this passage is about elements being burned on the earth's surface and in the sky (lower heavens) at Armageddon so the earth's surface, the atmosphere, and the sky will be set free, released, and loosed from all that presently pollutes and defiles it in order that creation will be purified and renewed for the millennial reign of Christ and His church.

## Emendation, "Burned Up"

In New Testament Greek 2 Peter 3:10 does not have the words "burned up." Rather, this verse ends abruptly with *heuriskomai*, meaning "will be found" or "will be exposed." Since the emendation "burned up" is not in the Greek text, scholars have appropriately added it to enable this sentence to read as good English and to clarify its meaning based on context. Common emendations for this verse in reference to man's works are: "will be burned up" (NASB); "will be exposed" (ESV); and "will be laid bare" (NIV). However, "'Various conjectural emendations have been proposed: ... (Olivier) 'will be **burnt to ashes;**' ... (Vansittart) 'will be burned.'"[14]

Although the emendation for 2 Peter 3:10 "will be burned up" is acceptable, the author proposes an emendation consistent with context for three reasons: (1) The immediate context of 2 Peter 2:6 says, "to ashes;" (2) The greater context of Scripture about Armageddon says, "The wicked; they will be **ashes** under the soles of your feet" (Malachi 4:3 NIV); and (3) Scholar Oliver has proposed the emendation, "will be burnt to ashes." Therefore, the proposed emendation for 2 Peter 3:10 in reference to man's works is: "will be found **burned to ashes.**"

## PROPOSED MORE LITERAL TRANSLATION

Based on this New Testament Greek word study the following is proposed as a more literal and accurate translation of 2 Peter 3:10-12:

> The day of the Lord will come like a thief, in which the lower heavens [corrupted by the Fall] will pass away with a loud cracking sound and the elements being burned will be set free, and on earth, its works will be found burned to ashes. These thusly all being set free in this way, what sort of people ought you to be in holy conduct and godliness, looking for and hastening the coming of the day of God, on account of which the lower heavens being on fire will be set free, and the elements will melt with intense heat! (2 Peter 3:10-12, Proposed).

Working with this more literal translation of 2 Peter 3:10-12 it is apparent that annihilation of the universe is not in view. Rather, what is being described is the Lord raining blazing fire on the entire earth's surface and throughout the lower heavens (sky) in order to purify and renew them in preparation for His millennial reign. Therefore, a literal translation of 2 Peter 3:10-12 supports a premillennial and not an amillennial position.

Now, let's do an exegesis of this passage.

## EXEGESIS OF 2 PETER 3:10-12

"The day of the Lord will come like a thief." Christ's return at Armageddon will be unexpected.

"The lower heavens will pass away with a loud cracking sound." The lower heavens — the atmosphere corrupted by the Fall and the curse upon it which causes it to produce tornadoes, floods, famines, and devastating hurricanes, and the sky immediately beyond corrupted by human activities such as satellite space debris—will pass away with a (Gk., *rhoizedon;* loud cracking sound) produced by intense heat as King Jesus cleanses the lower heavens with fire.

"The elements being burned will be set free." Contaminates in the lower heavens (the atmosphere and the sky immediately beyond) to include radioactive particles from stricken nuclear plants and likely future limited nuclear war, smog, and space debris will be burned with intense heat causing elements in these substances to be set free, and other elements reduced to ashes.

"On earth, its works will be found burned to ashes." All the works of man from casinos to castles will be burned to ashes.

"These thusly all being set free in this way, what sort of people ought you to be in holy conduct and godliness, looking for and hastening the coming of the day of God." Recognizing that everything that is on the earth's surface and in the lower heavens that are works of man will be burned with blazing fire, causing elements in these substances to be set free or reduced to ashes, what an incentive this is for us to conduct our lives in holiness and godliness as we look for and hasten the coming day of God at Armageddon.

"On account of which the lower heavens being on fire will be set free." The atmosphere and the sky immediately beyond, being on fire, will be set free from contaminates, radioactive particles, and space debris as Christ purifies the lower heavens with fire.

"Elements will melt with intense heat." Everything on the earth's surface from skyscrapers to sports cars, and everything in the sky from satellites to space debris will melt with intense heat as Christ at Armageddon purifies and renews the earth's surface and the lower heavens in preparation for His visible earthly millennial reign.

## DAWN OF THE MILLENNIUM

With our Lord Jesus Christ at Armageddon having accomplished what remained unfulfilled of Daniel's seventy weeks prophecy, having made improvements to earth's topography, having purified and renewed by fire the earth's surface and the sky (creation renovated and set free from its contaminants) in preparation for His millennial reign with His church, it is time now for the dawn of the millennium — the predicted blessing — as Ante-Nicene father Irenaeus remarks:

> The predicted blessing, therefore, belongs unquestionably to the times of the kingdom [the millennium], when the righteous shall bear rule upon their rising from the dead; when also the **creation, having been renovated and set free**, shall fructify with an abundance of all kinds of food.[15]

Although we call this upcoming restful time for the saints the millennium, Ante-Nicene fathers called it the "Sabbath rest for the people of God" (Hebrews 4:9).

But first, let's review the timeline of the seventieth week, the progression of events from the beginning of birth pains to Armageddon.

# 14

# TIMELINE OF THE SEVENTIETH WEEK

Many Christians today believe that the church will not be on earth during Daniel's seventieth week, the final seven years. However, this belief is just the opposite of what the Bible teaches, **because**:

Israel (both national and spiritual Israel) has one week, or seven years, to fulfill in order to complete Israel's allotted dispensation. According to Romans 11:17 the Gentile church was grafted into spiritual Israel "and became partaker with them of the rich root of the olive tree [Israel]," Christ Jesus having "made both groups into **one**" (Ephesians 2:14). Therefore, since spiritual Israel must absolutely be on the earth during Israel's seventieth week so they can complete Israel's dispensation, this means that the Gentile church that was grafted into spiritual Israel (Romans 11:17) must also absolutely be on the earth during the seventieth week, the final seven years, or the equivalent time thereof. (See Chapter 5 for more details).

On the other hand, early church premillennialists held that the church will be on the earth during the first two major events of the final seven years — the beginning of birth pains and the time, times, and half a time tribulation of persecution — but will be caught away (raptured) at the first phase return of Jesus Christ in the sky *before* the outpouring of the wrath of the Lamb judgments described in The Revelation.

Following is biblical and premillennial Ante-Nicene fathers' teachings of the timeline of the seventieth week, the final seven years, or 2,556 days:

## Start of the Seventieth Week (Day 1)

**Antichrist's Treaty with Israel**: "The prince [the Antichrist] who is to come ... will make a firm covenant with the many [Israel] for one week" (Daniel 9:27), starting the final seven years, the seventieth week.

**Beginning of Birth Pains** (also called the beginning of sorrows): Jesus said, "Many will come in my name, claiming, 'I am the Christ,' and will deceive many. You will hear of wars and rumors of wars, but see to it that you are not alarmed. Such things must happen, but the end is still to come. Nation will rise against nation, and kingdom against kingdom. There will be famines and earthquakes in various places. All these things are the beginning of birth pains" (Matthew 24:4-8 NIV). The birth pains described here have occurred for centuries; however, like birth pains that increase in frequency and intensity as the time to give birth draws near, so will these described as creation's birth pains.

## Beginning of Tribulation of Persecution

"In the **middle** of the week he [the Antichrist] will put a stop to [abolish] sacrifice and grain offering [in the Jerusalem Temple]" (Daniel 9:27), starting the tribulation.

Many believers interpret "middle" here as midpoint; however, middle can have a broader meaning. In ancient Israel the Jews had three night watches—first, middle, and last (Judges 7:19). The first watch was from 6 PM to 10 PM, the middle watch was from 10 PM to 2 AM, and the last watch was from 2 AM to 6 AM; three four-hour shifts. Therefore, applying this first, middle, and last model to the seventieth week of 2,556 days, "the middle of the week" can be any day between the 853rd to the 1,704th day when the Antichrist stops the Jerusalem Temple sacrifices, breaking his covenant and starting the tribulation.

Based on subsequent events, the likely start of the end of days tribulation of persecution is around day 1,070.

## ABOMINATION OF DESOLATION (ABOUT DAY 2,360)

Daniel said, "From the time that the regular sacrifice is abolished and the abomination of desolation is set up, there will be **1,290 days**" (Daniel 12:11). Therefore, from the start of the seventieth week (day 1) to the beginning of the tribulation around day 1,070 + 1,290 days = about day 2,360 for the **abomination** of desolation.

## GREAT TRIBULATION OF PERSECUTION (ABOUT DAY 2,360)

Jesus said, "When you see the abomination of desolation . . . then there will be a **great tribulation** [great persecution], such as has not occurred since the beginning of the world until now, nor ever will. Unless those days had been cut short, no [Christian] life would have been saved; but for the sake of the elect those days will be cut short" (Matthew 24:15, 16, 21, 22).

In Daniel, it was asked the angelic messenger, "'How long will it be until the end of these wonders?'" ". . . A **time, times, and half a time**; and as soon as they finish shattering the power of the holy people, all these events will be completed'" (vss. 12:6-7).

Daniel also said, "Blessed is he who waits and attains to the **1,335 days!**" (Daniel 12:12), or about 45 days more for great tribulation (1,290 + 45 = 1,335 days). The "1,335 days" for the tribulation period are equivalent to "a time, times, and half a time" (Daniel 12:7), or about "forty-two months" (Revelation 11:2; 13:5), or about three and one-half years (rounded) within the final seven years, the seventieth week.

Ante-Nicene father Tatian encourages the church:

> There shall be then great tribulation . . . but when these things begin to be, be of good cheer, and lift up your heads; for your salvation is come near.[1]

Early church bishop Hippolytus also remarks:

> The words, "Blessed is he that waiteth and cometh to the thousand three hundred and five and thirty [1,335] days,"

have also their value, as the Lord said: "But he that shall endure unto the end, the same shall be saved."[2]

Therefore, from the start of the seventieth week (day 1) to the beginning of the tribulation of persecution around day 1,070 + 1,290 days of initial tribulation + about 45 days more for great tribulation equal about day 2,405 when the tribulation period **ends**, but is uncertain because Jesus said "those days will be cut short" (Matthew 24:22).

## CHRIST'S RETURN, THE RESURRECTION AND RAPTURE

Jesus said, "Immediately *after* the tribulation of those days the sun will be darkened, and the moon will not give its light . . . and they will see **the Son of Man** [Jesus] **coming on the clouds** of the sky with power and great glory. And He will send forth His angels with a great trumpet and they will gather together His elect [His church] from the four winds, from one end of the sky to the other" (Matthew 24:29-31). This is Christ's *first phase* return *for* His church. Notice that there is no mention in this passage about Christ returning to earth at this point; He is only seen in the sky ingathering His elect, the whole company of the redeemed, the church.

"For the Lord Himself will descend from heaven with a shout, with the voice of the archangel and with the trumpet of God, and the dead in Christ will rise first. Then we who are alive and remain will be caught up together with them in the clouds to meet the Lord in the air, and so we shall always be with the Lord" (1 Thessalonians 4:16-17).

Upon Christ's first phase return and His gathering of the church in the sky by resurrection and rapture, Jesus, the Lamb of God, will justly repay the ungodly followers of Antichrist remaining on earth with His terrible wrath of the Lamb judgments.

The church is ushered into heaven (Revelation 7:9-17).

## WRATH OF THE LAMB JUDGMENTS ON EARTH

Followers of Antichrist left on earth will say "to the mountains and to the rocks, "Fall on us and hide us from the presence of Him who sits on the throne, and from the **wrath of the Lamb**; for the great day of their wrath has come, and who is able to stand?'" (Revelation 6:16,17).

With the opening of the seventh seal in Revelation 8, the judgments of the wrath of the Lamb begin. During these awful months an angel will open "the bottomless pit [the abyss]. . . . Then out of the smoke came locusts upon the earth, and power was given them, as the scorpions of the earth have power. . . . And they were not permitted to kill anyone, but to torment for **five months** [about 150 days]" (Revelation 9:2,3,5).

Therefore, from the start of the seventieth week (day 1) to the beginning of the tribulation of persecution around day 1,070 + 1,290 days of initial tribulation + about 45 days of great tribulation + about 150 days for the wrath of the Lamb judgments = around day 2,555.

This leaves one day for Armageddon.

## BATTLE OF ARMAGEDDON (DAY 2,556)

"And they gathered them together to the place called in Hebrew, **Armageddon**." (Revelation 16:16 NKJV).

Returning from heaven to earth to fight for the 144,000 or "all of the chosen thousands" of Messianic Christian Jews at Jerusalem, the armies in heaven were following Jesus, the King of kings, in Christ's *second phase* return *with* His church.

And, "the beast [the Antichrist] and the kings of the earth and their armies assembled to make war against Him. . . . And the beast was seized, and with him the false prophet; . . . these two were thrown alive into the lake of fire" (Revelation 19:19-20).

Therefore, from the start of the seventieth week (day 1) to the beginning of the tribulation of persecution around day 1,070 + 1,290 days of initial tribulation + about 45 days of great tribulation + about 150 days for the wrath of the Lamb judgments + 1 day for Armageddon = day 2,556 completing the final seven years, the seventieth week.

Dear saint, with Armageddon ended and the earth at rest, it's time to take a break—the "Sabbath rest for the people of God" (Hebrews 4:9).

## EARLY CHURCH PREM
Timeline of the Seventiet[

Tribulation Begins

Beginning of Birth Pains
(Matthew 24:8)

Tribulation of Persecution

1,290 Days (Daniel 12:11)

**Day 1** – Start of the 70th week (7 years; 2,556 days) Antichrist makes covenant with Israel (Daniel 9:27)

"These are the beginning of birth pains." (Matthew 24:8)

"In the middle [not the midpoint] of the week" (Daniel 9:27) the Antichrist breaks his covenant and abolishes sacrifices, starting the tribulation of persecution. Based on subsequent events, about Day 1,070.

**Tribulation period "a time, tin**
(Daniel 12:7), or about 3 ½ years, c
(Daniel 12:12
Antichrist rules the world 42 m

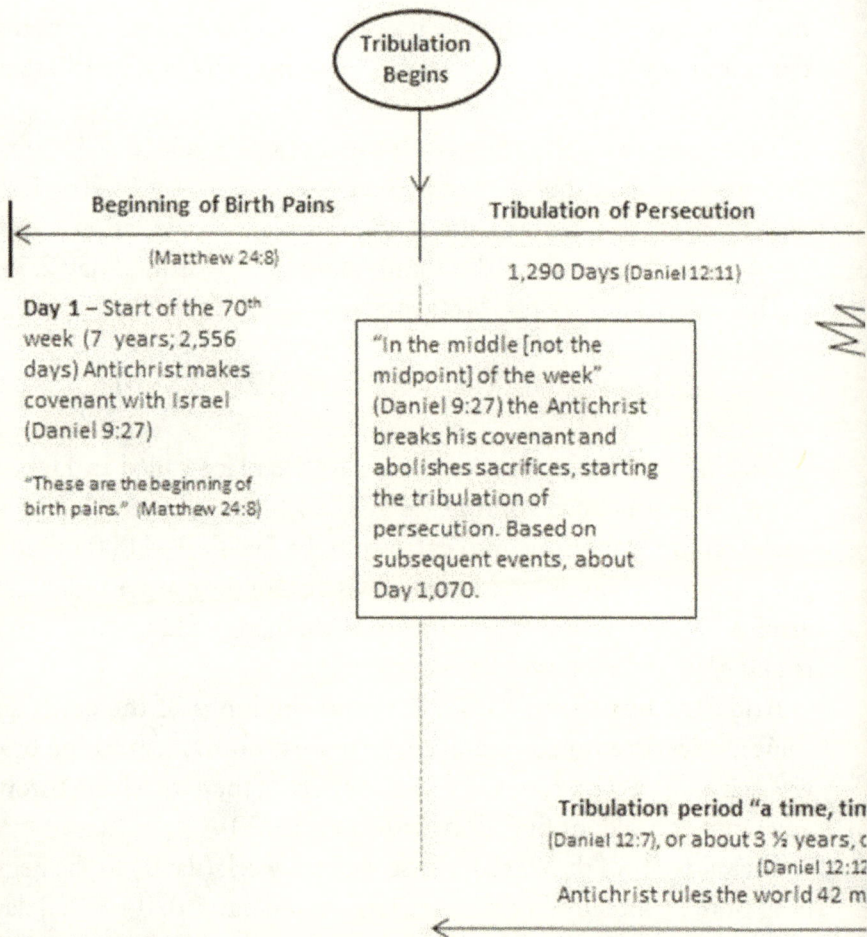

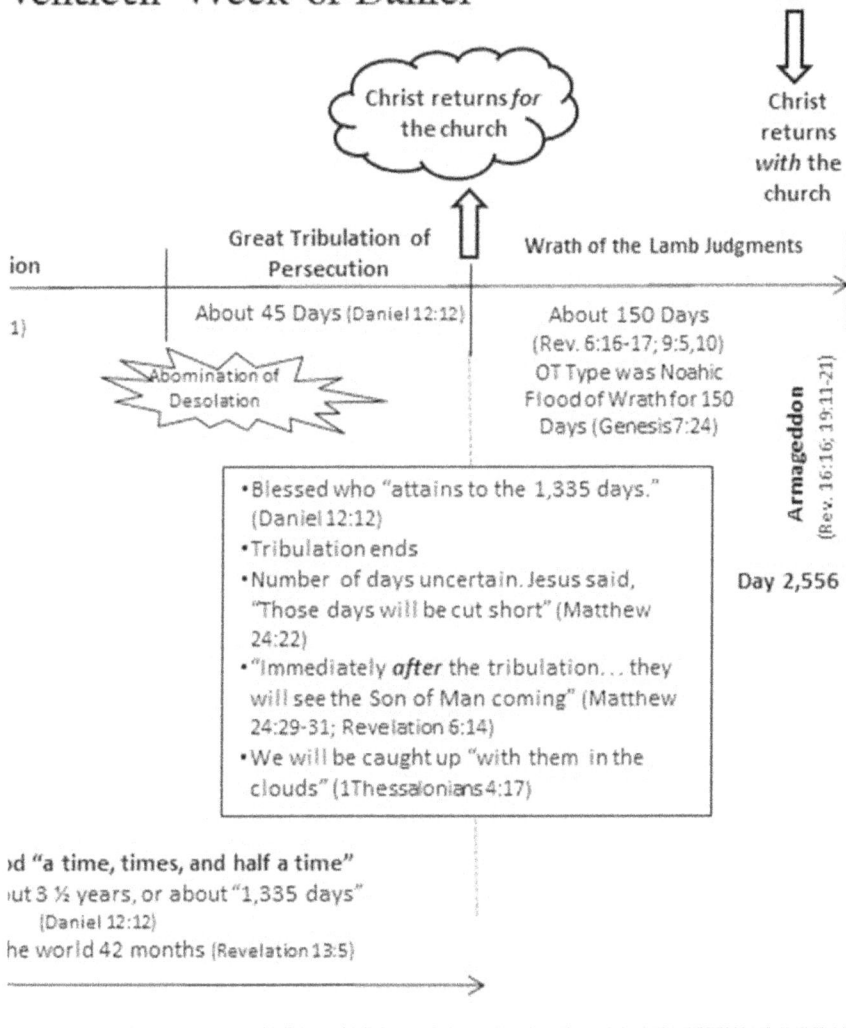

PREMILLENNIALISM
ventieth Week of Daniel

Christ returns *for* the church

Christ returns *with* the church

Great Tribulation of Persecution

Wrath of the Lamb Judgments

ion

1)

About 45 Days (Daniel 12:12)

About 150 Days (Rev. 6:16-17; 9:5,10) OT Type was Noahic Flood of Wrath for 150 Days (Genesis 7:24)

Abomination of Desolation

Armageddon (Rev. 16:16; 19:11-21)

Day 2,556

• Blessed who "attains to the 1,335 days." (Daniel 12:12)
• Tribulation ends
• Number of days uncertain. Jesus said, "Those days will be cut short" (Matthew 24:22)
• "Immediately *after* the tribulation... they will see the Son of Man coming" (Matthew 24:29-31; Revelation 6:14)
• We will be caught up "with them in the clouds" (1 Thessalonians 4:17)

d "a time, times, and half a time"
ut 3 ½ years, or about "1,335 days"
        (Daniel 12:12)
he world 42 months (Revelation 13:5)

# 15

# THE SABBATH REST

Need a break? God's people are about to enjoy some rest and relaxation.

In the Ante-Nicene era our ancestral parents in the faith used to call this upcoming time of rest and relaxation by its biblical name: The "Sabbath rest for the people of God" (Hebrews 4:9). Today, we call it the millennium.

The millennium has been a topic of debate in theological circles for . . . well, over a millennium. In this chapter you will discover the basis for the millennium, the questions about the millennium, and the conditions that will characterize the millennium as taught in Scripture and by early church premillennialists.

## BASIS FOR THE MILLENNIUM

It is often said that the only basis for the millennium (from Latin, *mille*, meaning thousand) is the passage Revelation 20:1-7. So, here it is:

> I saw an angel coming down out of heaven, having the key to the Abyss and holding in his hand a great chain. He seized the dragon, that ancient serpent, who is the devil, or Satan, and bound him for a thousand years. He threw him into the Abyss, and locked and sealed it over him, to keep him from

deceiving the nations anymore until the thousand years were ended. After that, he must be set free for a short time. I saw thrones on which were seated those who had been given authority to judge. And I saw the souls of those who had been beheaded because of their testimony for Jesus and because of the word of God. They had not worshiped the beast or his image and had not received his mark on their foreheads or their hands. They came to life and reigned with Christ a thousand years. (The rest of the dead did not come to life until the thousand years were ended.) This is the first resurrection. Blessed and holy are those who have part in the first resurrection. The second death has no power over them, but they will be priests of God and of Christ and will reign with him for a **thousand years**. When the thousand years are over, Satan will be released from his prison. (NIV)

Although many people today consider this passage the only basis for the millennium, early church premillennialists did not base their teachings about the millennium solely on Revelation 20. Instead, they based them primarily on the divine principle found initially in the first book of the Bible, the principle that God works six days and rests on the seventh day, as stated in the creation account:

By the seventh day God had finished the work he had been doing; so on the **seventh day he rested** from all his work. And God blessed the seventh day and made it holy, because on it he rested from all the work of creating that he had done. (Genesis 2:2-3 NIV)

This principle is found throughout Scripture, "You shall work six days, but on the seventh day you shall rest" (Exodus 34:21).

Based on this principle, early church premillennialists taught that when the days of work during this present evil age are complete, there will be a thousand-year seventh day of rest for the people of God. We call this period, the millennium, but they held that it will be the promised Sabbath rest, quoting Hebrews: "So there remains a Sabbath rest for the people of God" (vs. 4:9).

Consequently, early church premillennial Ante-Nicene fathers based their interpretations about the Sabbath rest on these verses that speak of a "thousand years" as a being one day with God:

> For a thousand years in your sight are like a day that has just gone by, or like a watch in the night (Psalm 90:4 NIV).

> But do not let this one fact escape your notice, beloved, that with the Lord a day is as a thousand years, and a thousand years as one day. (2 Peter 3:8)

Many people interpret these verses figuratively, but early church premillennialists interpreted them literally that in this age a thousand years are "as one day" with God. Hippolytus comments:

> Six thousand years must needs be accomplished, in order that the **Sabbath** may come, the **rest**, the holy day "on which God rested from all His works." For the Sabbath is the type and emblem of the future **kingdom** [the millennium] of the saints, when they "shall **reign with Christ**," when He comes from heaven, as John says in his Apocalypse: for "a day with the Lord is as a thousand years." Since, then, in six days God made all things, it follows that **six thousand years** must be fulfilled. And they are not yet fulfilled.[1]

Concerning the six thousand years, a well-known minister seen regularly on television calculated the number of years that has elapsed during this present evil age. He began his calculation with the creation of Adam. Then, he added recorded biblical history (e.g., the age of fathers when children were born to them, the reigns of kings, etc.) that has since elapsed. He calculated that six thousand years was exceeded in the 1990's.

But there is one major error with his calculation: this present evil age did **not** begin with the creation of Adam. Adam and later Eve were created holy. They walked with God. They were sinless. This present evil age began, not with the creation of Adam, but with the Fall.

**151**

## How Old Was Adam When He Fell Into Sin?

The Bible does not tell us Adam's age when he disobeyed God and ate of the tree of the knowledge of good and evil (Genesis 3:6). However, the Bible gives us clues.

After the Fall, Adam and Eve were driven by God out of the Garden. Then, Adam had relations with his wife, Eve, and she gave birth to their first son, Cain (Genesis 4:1). Later, his brother, Abel, was born. These boys, Cain and Abel, grew up and tended crops and livestock on the family farm. Eventually, however, Cain became angry with Abel and murdered him. After Cain killed Abel, Cain moved away (Genesis 4:16). Later on, Adam and Eve's third son was born named Seth. Adam was **130 years old** when Seth was born (Genesis 5:3). In the pre-flood environment, people lived longer.

Now, flashback to the Fall.

How old was Cain when he murdered his brother? Was he maybe 20, 40, 70 years old? Add to that, time for their third son, Seth, to be born. Whatever is the total number of those years, subtract it from Adam's age of 130 years when Seth was born to him and that will approximate the age of Adam when he fell into sin—the starting point for this present evil age.

Although six thousand years since the creation of Adam has likely elapsed, it is also possible that six thousand years since the Fall of Adam into sin has **not** elapsed.

According to early church premillennialists, when the six thousand years of this present evil age are complete, then the Sabbath rest millennium will begin in the seventh millenary of years, as Ante-Nicene father Victorinus wrote:

> That true and just **Sabbath** should be observed in the **seventh millenary** of years. Wherefore to those seven days the Lord attributed to each a thousand years; for thus went the warning: "In Thine eyes, O Lord, a thousand years are as one day." Therefore ... that true Sabbath will be in the seventh millenary of years, when Christ with His elect shall reign [the millennium].[2]

Yet, are God's days in this present evil age really thousand year days? Irenaeus answers this question in the affirmative citing the account of Adam who lived to be 930 years old (Genesis 5:4).

> Since "a day of the Lord is as a thousand years," he [Adam] did not overstep the thousand years, but died within them, thus bearing out the sentence of his sin. . . . He did not overstep the thousand years, but died within their limit,—it follows that, in regard to all these significations, God is indeed true.[3]

God had told Adam that if he ate of the tree of the knowledge of good and evil "in the day that you eat from it you will surely die" (Genesis 2:17). Thus, it is Irenaeus' opinion that Adam and Eve and their sinful descendants have never seen the light of a second day, meaning God's day based on the Ante-Nicene interpretation of Psalm 90:4 and 2 Peter 3:8 that a thousand years in this present evil age is one day with God. "God is indeed true,"[4] says Irenaeus.

## Does God Measure Time the Same in All Ages?

During the creation week God apparently measured His days like that of man, twenty-four hours per day, based on the rotation of the earth. "For there was evening and there was morning, one day" (Genesis 1:5). At creation, God and man dwelt in harmony. But, after the Fall, God and man were estranged. Did God continue to measure His days the same as man, then? The Bible doesn't say. But early church premillennialists were absolutely convinced that God's days in this present evil age are thousand-year days, as Ante-Nicene father Lactantius wrote:

> Since all the works of God were completed in **six days**, the world must continue in its present state through . . . six thousand years. . . . As the prophet shows, who says "In Thy sight, O Lord, a thousand years are as one day." And as God laboured during those six days in creating such great works, so His religion and truth must labour during these

**six thousand years**, while wickedness prevails and bears rule. And again, since God, having finished His works, rested the seventh day and blessed it, at the end of the six thousandth year all wickedness must be abolished from the earth, and righteousness reign for a thousand years [the millennium]; and there must be tranquility and rest from the labours which the world now has long endured.[5]

Lactantius declares that the thousand years of millennial rest (one Lord's day) follows six thousand years of work (six Lord's days) during this present age "while wickedness prevails."[6]

In other words, early church premillennialists taught according to a literal interpretation of the Bible that the millennium, or "Sabbath rest for the people of God" (Hebrews 4:9), is future. They also held that during the future Sabbath rest millennium that "Christ with His elect shall reign."[7]

Thus, early church premillennialists taught according to a literal interpretation of the Scriptures that Jesus Christ will return *before* the millennium (premillennialism).

Still, prophecies about the millennium pose fascinating questions.

## QUESTIONS ABOUT THE MILLENNIUM

In coffee shop gatherings for Bible study, principal questions asked about the millennium are: What will be the identity of people on earth during the millennium? Where will animals come from during the millennium? Will there be people in fleshly bodies during the millennium? And, will both resurrected and non-resurrected people be on earth during the millennium?

### The Identity of People on Earth During the Millennium

Dispensational premillennialists contend that the church and Israel are distinct, and further claim that the church is heavenly and that her home is in heaven, but that Israel is earthly and that her home is on earth. Thus, they claim that the identity of the people on earth during the millennium will be a regathered national Israel.

Yet, Scripture is clear that Gentile believers were grafted into Israel (Romans 11:17), and that Jesus Christ has "made both groups into one" (Ephesians 2:14). For this reason, early church and historic premillennialists both hold that the identity of the people on earth during the millennium will be "the Israel of God" (Galatians 6:16). That is, spiritual Israel, which includes the grafted in Gentile believers and the grafted in newly believing 144,000 or "all of the chosen thousands" of modern national Israel, whom altogether comprise the whole company of the redeemed, Jew and Gentile, "the body of Christ" (1 Corinthians 12:27), "the elect" (2 Timothy 2:10), "the saints" (1 Corinthians 14:33), "the church" (Ephesians 1:22).

Moreover, the Bible tells us the identity of the people on earth during the millennium:

> Thou [Jesus] wast slain, and didst purchase for God with Thy blood from **every tribe, and people, and nation** [the church, Jew and Gentile]; and Thou hast made us a kingdom [millennial kingdom] unto our God, and hast made us priests, and **they shall reign upon the earth**. (Revelation 5:9,10)

### Where Will Animals Come From During the Millennium?

This goes to the power of God and whether we believe He can do what He says He will do and has proven himself easily capable of doing in the past. During the flood the Lord saved clean animals in sets of seven, male and female. He did the same for the birds. From the unclean animals, He saved them in pairs, male and female (Genesis 7:2,3).

If the Lord can save animals, birds, and all sorts of crawling things through the Flood (Genesis 7:14-16), if the Lord can save three Hebrews, Shadrach, Meshach and Abednego after being tossed alive into Nebuchadnezzar's furnace of blazing fire such that when they came out the hair on their heads was not even singed nor was even the smell of smoke on them (Daniel 3:27), and if the Lord can save believing fleshly bodied Jews from modern national Israel through the fire at Armageddon, then we need not to be too concerned about the Lord, the Creator, protecting some animals, birds, and all sorts of crawling things through the Armageddon fire so they can populate the earth during the millennium.

## People in Fleshly Bodies During the Millennium?

Early church and modern dispensational premillennialists both hold that people will dwell in fleshly bodies during the millennium. Early church premillennialists held that these people in their flesh will be the newly believing 144,000 or "all of the chosen thousands" of national Israel who will be in their flesh when King Jesus returns with the church at Armageddon to fight for Israel. Christ will protect them from the Armageddon fire (Isaiah 43:2-3), and they will remain on earth in their fleshly bodies during the millennium.

But what about the Scripture: "Flesh and blood cannot inherit the kingdom of God" (1 Corinthians 15:50)? In response, during our Lord's earthly ministry He revealed to a crowd. "The kingdom of God is in your midst" (Luke 17:21). In other words, the crowd of flesh and blood people contained people who loved and served the Lord and who belonged to the kingdom of God, while other people in the crowd did not love and serve the Lord and who did not belong to the kingdom of God. As was the case then, all people on earth today who belong to the kingdom of God have bodies of flesh and blood.

The question is, at what point in time was Paul referring when he said, "Flesh and blood cannot inherit the kingdom of God (1 Corinthians 15:50)? He explains when: "Behold, I tell you a mystery; we will not all sleep, but we will all be changed, in a moment, in the twinkling of an eye, at the last trumpet; for the trumpet will sound, and the dead will be raised imperishable, and we will be changed" (1 Corinthians 15:51-52)? He was referring to the time of the resurrection and rapture of the church at Christ's return in the sky.

Nonetheless, when Christ returns with the church months later at Armageddon the newly believing 144,000 or "all of the chosen thousands" of modern national Israel on earth will be in their fleshly bodies, like believers today. Regarding them, Old Testament prophecy indicates that they will enter the millennium in their flesh and will bear children (Isaiah 11:8). Lactantius held that these people will receive their immortal bodies <u>after</u> the millennium, saying:

> When the thousand years [millennium] shall be completed, the world shall be renewed by God, and the heavens shall be folded together, and the earth shall be changed, and God shall transform men [and women of national Israel in their fleshly bodies] into the similitude of angels.[8]

However, it should be noted that the Bible does not state when these believing men and women of national Israel in their fleshly bodies during the millennium will receive their immortal bodies, but one interpretation is that they will receive them after the millennium, when the present earth and heaven flee away at Revelation 20:11 in preparation for the creation of the new heaven and new earth when our Lord makes "all things new" (Revelation 21:5).

## Resurrected and Non-Resurrected People

One interesting bone of contention deserves attention. Some think it would be a problem to have both resurrected and non-resurrected people on earth during the millennium. But, since the resurrected Jesus conversed with His non-resurrected followers on a number of occasions, and once in their presence He ate "a piece of broiled fish" (Luke 24:43), this point seems moot.

During the millennium resurrected saints will be "like angels and are children of God, being children of the resurrection" (Luke 20:36 NRSV). Logically then, being like angels, the saints of the resurrection will likely enjoy the going back and forth between earth and heaven, whereas fleshly bodied believers of national Israel will dwell only on earth. These fleshly-bodied Messianic Jews, as well as saints of the resurrection, "will plant vineyards . . . [and] gardens and eat their fruit" (Amos 9:14 NIV), and enjoy other delightful conditions of the millennium.

## Conditions During the Millennium

Conditions that will characterize the Sabbath rest millennium are much different from what fallen man has experienced for about the last six millennia. The Bible describes the earth during the millennium as being restored by Jesus Christ to a state much as existed before the Fall. Some millennial promises are:

### Curse Lifted and the Earth Produces Bountifully

> The wilderness and the desert will be glad, and the Arabah will rejoice and blossom; like the crocus it will blossom profusely. . . . For waters will break forth in the wilderness and streams in the Arabah. The **scorched land** will become a pool and the thirsty ground springs of water (Isaiah 35:1, 2, 6, 7). Behold, days are coming, declares the Lord, when the plowman will overtake the reaper and the treader of grapes him who sows seed; when the mountains will drip sweet wine. (Amos 9:13)

Ante-Nicene father Papias, a contemporary of apostle John, wrote of an account told to him by church elders, who were told by St. John that the Lord related this to His disciples about the millennium:

> The days will come in which vines shall grow, having each ten thousand branches, and in each branch ten thousand twigs, and in each true twig ten thousand shoots, and in every one of the shoots ten thousand clusters, and on every one of the clusters ten thousand grapes. . . . Apples, and seeds, and grass would produce in similar proportions; and that all animals, feeding then only on the productions of the earth, would become peaceable and harmonious, and be in perfect subjection to man.[9]

## Satan, the Demons, and the Ungodly in the Abyss

Isaiah foretold that the Lord at Armageddon will imprison the ungodly in the abyss:

> So it will happen in that day, that the Lord will punish the host of heaven on high, and the kings of the earth on earth. They will be gathered together like prisoners in the dungeon, and will be confined in prison [the abyss]; and **after many days** they will be punished (Isaiah 24:21-22).

Apostle John clarifies the duration:

> Then I saw an angel coming down from heaven, holding the key of the abyss and a great chain in his hand. And he laid hold of the dragon, the serpent of old, who is the devil and Satan, and bound him for **a thousand years**; and he threw him into the abyss, and shut it and sealed it over him, so that he would not deceive the nations any longer, until the thousand years were completed; after these things he must be released for a short time. (Revelation 20:1-3)

Amillennialists believe that the great white throne final judgment — when the ungodly are sentenced to punishment in the lake of fire — occurs at Armageddon. However, Isaiah wrote about Armageddon and foretold at that time the ungodly will be confined in prison (the abyss), and then "after many days they will be punished" (Isaiah 24:22). In the progressive revelation of Scripture the New Testament clarifies "after many days" for the time of their punishment as being after "a thousand years" (Revelation 20:5).

## Jesus Christ Will Be King Over the Whole Earth

Zechariah the prophet wrote:

> The Lord will be **king over the whole earth**. On that day there will be one Lord, and his name the only name (v. 14:9 NIV).

Apostle Luke adds:

> He will be great and will be called the Son of the Most
> High. The Lord God will give him the throne of his father
> David, and he will reign over the house of Jacob forever; his
> kingdom will never end. (vss. 1:32-33 NIV)

## Followers of Jesus Christ Will Reign with Him

Scripture teaches that we will reign with Christ:

> It is a trustworthy statement: For if we died with Him, we
> will also live with Him; if we endure, we will also **reign** with
> Him (2 Timothy 2-11-12). You have made them to be a
> kingdom and priests to our God; and they will reign upon
> the earth. (Revelation 5:10)

## We Will Learn from Christ

Scripture also foretells that Jesus will teach us, probably much like
He taught ancient Jews along the Sea of Galilee:

> It will come about that in the last days the mountain of the
> house of the Lord will be established as the chief of the
> mountains, and will be raised above the hills; and all the
> nations will stream to it. And many peoples will come and
> say, "Come, let us go up to the mountain of the Lord, to the
> house of the God of Jacob; that He may **teach us** concern-
> ing His ways and that we may walk in His paths." For the
> law will go forth from Zion and the word of the Lord from
> Jerusalem. And He will judge between the nations, and will
> render decisions for many peoples. (Isaiah 2:2-4)

## Israel Will Be Restored to Her Promised Land

Millennium Messianic Jews will rebuild their cities:

> I will bring back my exiled people Israel; they will rebuild

the ruined cities and live in them. They will plant vineyards and drink their wine; they will make gardens and eat their fruit. I will plant Israel in their own land, never again to be uprooted from the land I have given them, says the Lord your God. (Amos 9:14-15 NIV)

## Wars Will Cease

After the Fall of man into sin, two brothers engaged in war, Cain and Abel. Today, according to *Wars in the World Daily News* there are sixty countries involved in wars. But when Jesus Christ reigns on the earth with His church, wars will cease:

He makes **wars to cease** to the end of the earth; He breaks the bow and cuts the spear in two; He burns the chariots with fire (Psalm 46:9). They will beat their swords into plowshares and their spears into pruning hooks. Nation will not take up sword against nation, nor will they train for war anymore. (Isaiah 2:4 NIV)

## Man and Animals Will Dwell in Peace

The Bible foretells that animals during the millennium will be at peace with man:

The wolf will live with the lamb, the leopard will lie down with the goat, the calf and the lion and the yearling together; and a little child will lead them. The cow will feed with the bear, their young will lie down together, and the lion will eat straw like the ox. The infant will play near the hole of the cobra, and the young child put his hand into the viper's nest. They will neither harm nor destroy on all my holy mountain, for the earth will be full of the knowledge of the Lord as the waters cover the sea. (Isaiah 11:6-9 NIV)

These Bible promises about conditions during the millennium seem almost fanciful because in this present evil age the only world conditions we have ever known are war, hunger, violent storms, devastating earthquakes, torrential floods, droughts, disease and death. We think these conditions are normal. But these sinful state conditions are abnormal in God's plan while millennium prophecies are normal in God's plan. And they will be fulfilled when Christ returns to this earth and restores our planet's condition to its original, intended order.

Now, with Israel having returned to her homeland to fulfill her seventieth week and her millennial prophecies, the start of the millennium may not be far away. So, be patient and wait for the angelic announcement—Welcome to the Millennium: The Sabbath Rest for the People of God.

But a word of caution! After the thousand years Satan will be released from the abyss and his ungodly troops will storm the camp of the saints. It will be the war to end all wars.

# 16

# THE ATTACK OF GOG AND MAGOG

*When the thousand years are completed, Satan will be released*
*from his prison [in the abyss], and will come out to deceive*
*the nations which are in the four corners of the earth, Gog and*
*Magog, to gather them together for the war; the number of*
*them is like the sand of the seashore. And they came up on the*
*broad plain of the earth and surrounded the camp of the saints*
*and the beloved city.*
*(Revelation 20:7-9)*

When H. G. Wells published his classic work about World War I, *The War That Will End War* (1914), he was obviously optimistic. Although his book promoted the idea that World War I would be "The War to End All Wars," the truth is, as long as the arch-deceiver Satan roams the earth there will be war.

During the millennium when this arch-deceiver is locked in the abyss, wars will "cease to the end of the earth" (Psalm 46:9). But after the thousand years, Satan will be released from his prison and will proceed to deceive the nations, "**Gog and Magog**, to gather them together for the war" (Revelation 20:8). Lactantius, in one of the few comments in Ante-Nicene writings about this war, remarks:

This [millennial] kingdom of the righteous shall be for a thousand years. Throughout that time the stars shall be more brilliant, and the brightness of the sun shall be increased, and the moon shall not be subject to decrease. Then the rain of blessing shall descend from God at morning and evening, and the earth shall bring forth all her fruit without the labour of men. Honey shall drop from rocks, fountains of milk and wine shall abound. The beasts shall lay aside their ferocity and become mild, the wolf shall roam among the flocks without doing harm, the calf shall feed with the lion, the dove shall be united with the hawk . . . no animal shall live by bloodshed. For God shall supply to all abundant and harmless food. But **when the thousand years shall be fulfilled, and the prince of the demons** [Satan] **loosed**, the nations will rebel against the righteous, and an innumerable multitude will come to storm the city of the saints.[1]

This predicted post-millennium attack by Gog and Magog on the saints encamped at the beloved city, Jerusalem, will be the real—War to End All Wars! Since all believers in Christ will participate in this last great war, you need to know about the identity of Satan's Gog and Magog troops, the state of millennium saints, and the attack and doom of Gog and Magog.

## IDENTITY OF SATAN'S GOG AND MAGOG TROOPS

Magog was the grandson of Noah (Genesis 10:2), born to Noah's son Japheth. Settling in an area north of Israel called the land of Magog, Magog and his descendants grew into an ancient nation.

Gog was a ruler "of the land of Magog, and prince of [the ancient territories] Rosh, Meshech, and Tubal" (Ezekiel 38:2). Therefore, in Revelation 20:7-9, the great company of Gog and Magog troops who come to attack the camp of the saints refer primarily to ancient people and not to people born during the millennium.

Who were these ancient people?

It should be noted that two events occur at the end of the millennium. First, Satan is released from the abyss "when the thousand years are completed" (Revelation 20:7). And secondly, the spirits of the ungodly with Satan in the abyss are resurrected back to life on earth at the millennium's end. As Apostle John wrote, "The rest of the [spiritual] dead did not come to life until the thousand years were completed" (Revelation 20:5).

Based on this testimony from Scripture, the *Exegetical Dictionary of the New Testament* comments on the identity of Gog and Magog troops in Revelation 20:7-9 who come to attack the saints:

> It is very possible that "the nations which are at the four corners of the earth, that is, Gog and Magog" (v. 8), are thought of as ... the [resurrected spiritual] dead, the troops of the world below.[2]

We may not think of the abyss as having nations of spirits of spiritually dead, ungodly people. But Jesus tells us that the majority of fallen humanity will die spiritually lost. He says, "Wide is the gate and broad is the road that leads to destruction, and **many** enter through it. But small is the gate and narrow the road that leads to life, and only a **few** find it" (Matthew 7:13,14 NIV). In other words, only a minority of the human race will turn from sin to follow Jesus Christ as their Savior and find eternal life. The majority will reject Jesus, His free gift of salvation, and will be assigned to the abyss.

These nations in the world below include ancient people like Gog and Magog. Since Gog and Magog literally and figuratively refer to ancient people it is reasonably conclusive that "Gog and Magog" troops in Revelation 20:8 are primarily post-millennium resurrected spiritually dead ungodly people who lived as far back as near the Flood, but would be inclusive of ungodly people who lived before and after.

Many Christians identify Satan's "Gog and Magog" troops in Revelation 20:8 as being disobedient Jews of national Israel born during the millennium. But note what Isaiah says concerning people on earth during the millennium: "They will hammer their swords into plowshares" (2:4). Therefore, it is unlikely that Satan's multitude of Gog and Magog troops whose number "is like the sand of the seashore" (Revelation 20:8) will comprise only people born during the millennium.

## Millennium Saints Flock to Jerusalem

When the millennium draws to a close and this war looms, the saints will flock to Jerusalem where our Savior and King Jesus will reign (Isaiah 2:2-3). There, Christ's people will camp at the beloved city while they await the attack of Gog and Magog.

Although this Gog and Magog attack on the saints and the beloved city are briefly described in Revelation 20:7-9, Ezekiel 38-39 provides details.

## Some Refrain from Going to Jerusalem

Unfortunately, even though saints are flocking to Jerusalem as the thousand years nears completion, we find in Ezekiel 38:13 that some people will refrain from traveling to the beloved city to camp with the saints. These are residents of "Sheba [in southern ancient Judah] and Dedan [in the Arabian Peninsula] and the merchants of Tarshish [on the shores of the Mediterranean] with all its villages."

The question is: Why are these millennium people not at Jerusalem with the saints?

Furthermore, these people are described as inquiring of Gog, asking him or his representative: "Have you come to capture spoil? Have you assembled your company to seize plunder, to carry away silver and gold, to take away cattle and goods, to capture great spoil?" (Ezekiel 38:13). Concerning them and their inquiry *The Pulpit Commentary* remarks:

> All are depicted as following in the wake of Gog ... inquiring whether Gog had come simply for the purpose of destruction or in the hope of trading with the booty he should capture. In this case they intimate their wish to be partakers of the spoil.[3]

Thus, there is evidence from Scripture that there will likely be disobedient Jews of national Israel born during the millennium who will fall away in their affections toward our Lord and King Jesus Christ such that they will not even go up to His throne. And by their wandering from the Master's side they fall prey to the devil's guile when he comes out of the abyss "to deceive the nations ... to gather them together for the war" (Revelation 20:8).

Therefore, in Revelation 20:7-9 it is reasonably conclusive, based on the broader context of Scripture, that the identity of Satan's Gog and Magog troops are both ancient resurrected spiritually dead ungodly people who come out of the abyss and back on earth in their flesh with Satan at the completion of "the thousand years" (Revelation 20:5), and disobedient Jews of national Israel born during the millennium who join this vast company from "the nations" of the world below (Isaiah 14:9). Together they comprise the whole company of the wicked of all the ages who come to do what they have been doing since Cain slew Abel—attack the saints and the Lord Jesus to destroy us—"the number of them is like the sand of the seashore" (Revelation 20:8).

## STATE OF MILLENNIUM SAINTS

Ezekiel foretells that when Gog and his vast army descend on Israel they will find a people "who are at rest, that live securely, all of them living without walls and having no bars or gates" (Ezekiel 38:11). "At rest" describes the tranquil state the saints will enjoy during the "Sabbath rest for the people of God" (Hebrews 4:9), the millennium.

As was common in the ancient world and is common today in the Middle East, houses are surrounded by fortified perimeter property walls. Ancient cities also had these walls, e.g. the wall of Jericho and the Jerusalem Wall, to protect from invaders, thieves, and wild animals. But, during the peaceful state of the millennium, the saints will dwell in harmony and animals will be tame. Thus, millennium saints will enjoy a state free from harm from man or beast and will have no protective walls, bars or gates.

In addition, during the millennium the saints will "live at the center of the world" (Ezekiel 38:12); that is, in the region of Israel's ancient homeland. But when the thousand years draw to a close, the saints will camp at Jerusalem for two reasons: One, with Jerusalem having risen in elevation a thousand years earlier at Armageddon (Zechariah 14:10), the post-millennium saints will have a vantage point at Jerusalem to scan the horizon for the approach of Satan's Gog and Magog troops. And, secondly, Jerusalem "is the city of the Great King" (Matthew 5:35 NIV), and the saints who love the Lord will want to be as close to our Great King Jesus as possible when Satan's Gog and Magog troops are spotted on the horizon—"all of them wielding swords (Ezekiel 38:4).

## ATTACK AND DOOM OF GOG AND MAGOG

Gog, the ruler of the land of Magog and prince of Rosh, Meshech, and Tubal, an elder prince of the underworld ruled by Satan, will lead the vast Gog and Magog multinational army. His forthcoming generalship, according to Ezekiel's prophecy, has been known to Gog for some time. He, having lived, ruled, died, and been removed to the abyss about four thousand years ago, Gog is aware that "After many days you will be summoned; in the latter years you will come into the land that is restored from the sword, whose inhabitants have been gathered from many nations to the mountains of Israel" (Ezekiel 38:8). At last, Gog's time will come and the Lord will bring him out with all his army.

Ezekiel prophesies, thus says the Lord God to Gog: "I will turn you about and put hooks into your jaws, and I will bring you out, and all your army" (Ezekiel 38:4). This is a good translation but the literal Hebrew is more explanatory as noted by *The Hebrew Bible: Andersen-Forbes Analyzed Text* which translates key sections of this verse: "I shall bring **back** and . . . I shall bring **out**."Thus, if Gog's army were predominantly disobedient people born during the millennium the expected language would be "I will bring down" from the north. However, the literal Hebrew implies that Gog will be brought **back** (as with resurrection) and that he will be brought **out** (as out of the abyss), and all his army. Thus, the literal Hebrew supports Gog's troops being predominantly the resurrected spiritual dead.

Ezekiel foretold of Gog's vast army that they will come "like a storm; you shall be like a cloud covering the land, you and all your troops, and many peoples with you" (Ezekiel 38:9 NRSV). Although Gog is their General, Ezekiel says thoughts come into his mind, evidently from Satan, so that he devises an evil plan:

> It will come about on that day, that thoughts will come into your mind and you will devise an evil plan, and you will say, "I will go up against the land of unwalled villages. I will go against those who are at rest, that live securely, all of them living without walls and having no bars or gates, to capture spoil and to seize plunder, to turn your hand against the waste places which are now inhabited, and against the people who are gathered from the nations, who have acquired cattle and goods, who live at the center of the world." (Ezekiel 38:10-12)

From outward appearance, Gog's victory is sure. The millennium saints have no fortifications, no bars, no gates, and no weapons (Ezekiel 38:11; Isaiah 2:4).

But for Gog, and his army, defeat, not victory, is certain.

Ezekiel says "all your army, horses and horsemen, all of them [will be] splendidly attired, a great company with buckler and shield, all of them wielding swords" (v. 4).

It may be asked: If Gog's vast army is predominantly resurrected spiritual dead, where do they obtain swords and shields? The same could be asked if his army was mostly disobedient people born during the millennium. Would people at rest during the millennium build manufacturing plants to produce swords and shields sufficient to equip an army whose troops number as "the sand of the seashore," and all this under the watchful omnipresent eye of King Jesus who will reign on the earth during the millennium? Highly unlikely!

On the other hand, we should not discount the power of the fallen cherub to equip his army.

Before the exodus of the Jews from Egypt, Moses and Aaron appeared before Pharaoh, who told them to perform a miracle. So, "Aaron threw his staff down before Pharaoh and his servants, and it became a serpent" (Exodus 7:10). Not to be outdone, Pharaoh called his Satanic empowered sorcerers and magicians and "each one threw down his staff and they turned into serpents" (Exodus 7:12). Thus, we should not discount Satan's supernatural power to equip Gog's army, "a great company with buckler and shield, all of them wielding swords" (Ezekiel 38:4).

As General Gog and his troops come within sight of Jerusalem "all of them riding on horses, a great assembly and a mighty army" (Ezekiel 38:15), he and his troops will suppose that the saints camped at Jerusalem will be easy prey.

But Gog will have miscalculated when it comes to the saints' General — the Almighty Lord and King Jesus Christ. The saints will call upon Him, perhaps with the prayer of the Psalmist: "The Lord is my rock and my fortress and my deliverer, my God, my rock, in whom I take refuge; my shield and the horn of my salvation, my stronghold. I call upon the Lord, who is worthy to be praised, and I am saved from my enemies" (Psalm 18:2,3).

In answer to the prayers of His people, His inspired prophets foretell what will happen when our Lord goes forth in His fury to defend His holy saints:

> "It will come about on that day, when Gog comes against the land of Israel," declares the Lord God, "that My fury will mount up in My anger. In My zeal and in My blazing wrath I declare that on that day there will surely be a great earthquake in the land of Israel. The fish of the sea, the birds of the heavens, the beasts of the field, all the creeping things that creep on the earth, and all the men who are on the face of the earth will shake at My presence. . . . With pestilence and with blood I will enter into judgment with him; and I will rain on him and on his troops, and on the many peoples who are with him, a torrential rain, with hailstones, fire and brimstone" (Ezekiel 38:18-20, 22). [They will] "fall on the mountains of Israel . . . and I [the Lord] will send fire upon Magog." (Ezekiel 39:4, 6)

The number of them is like the sand of the seashore. And they came up on the broad plain of the earth and surrounded the camp of the saints and the beloved city, and fire came down from heaven and devoured them. And the devil who deceived them was thrown into the lake of fire [and likely also at this time the demons who served him]. (Revelation 20:9-10)

What happens to Gog and his troops, predominantly the nations of the wicked from the world below, who come out to attack the saints and the beloved city and are devoured by fire from heaven? God says, "I will give Gog a burial place there in Israel . . . they will bury Gog and all his multitude" (Ezekiel 39:11 NKJV). The Psalmist also reveals:

The wicked will return to Sheol [the netherworld or abyss], even all the nations who forget God. (Psalm 9:17)

Ante-Nicene father Lactantius adds, "Then the righteous shall go forth from their hiding places . . . but the whole race of the wicked shall utterly perish."[4] And the end will have come for . . . The War to End All Wars.
Then, in God's time, will appear a great white throne.

# 17

# EARTH AND HEAVEN DISAPPEAR

*And I saw a great white throne and Him who sat upon it,*
*from whose presence earth and heaven fled away [Gk., ephugen,*
*quickly disappeared] and no place was found for them.*
*(Revelation 20:11)*

According to Scripture, when a great white throne appears, earth and heaven will mysteriously disappear quickly! How can this happen? Does the Bible give us insight into how earth and heaven will quickly disappear, as well as what transpires during the subsequent great white throne judgment? Indeed, it does.

## HOW DO EARTH AND HEAVEN QUICKLY DISAPPEAR?

As mentioned, amillennialists have long thought that earth and heaven will be burned up and totally destroyed at Armageddon based on their interpretation of 2 Peter 3:10-12. But, as discussed in Chapter 10, Lavoisier's discovery in 1694 scientifically disproved that theory.

So, how do earth and heaven quickly disappear (i.e. annihilation of the universe) so a new earth and a new heaven can be created (Revelation 21:1)? The Bible explains.

## When Earth and Heaven Quickly Disappear

According to the Bible, a thousand years after Armageddon Satan will be released from the abyss and the spiritual dead will be resurrected back to life on earth. Then all the wicked will attack the camp of the saints during the Gog and Magog War (Revelation 20:5, 7, 8). After this, Revelation 20:11 says that he "saw a great white throne and Him [Jesus] who sat upon it, from whose presence earth and heaven fled away (Gk., *ephugen* from *pheugo*; vanished suddenly, fled away, **quickly disappeared**).

Thus, at Revelation 20:11 the present earth and heaven quickly disappear.

How is it possible that earth and heaven can quickly disappear? Well, the Bible gives us insight into this and quantum physicists explain the rest.

The Bible reveals "that the universe was formed at God's command, so that **what is seen was not made out of what was visible**" (Hebrews 11:3 NIV). In other words, the physical universe (all matter) was made out of the "invisible."

## Quantum Physics

Quantum physicists explain the world of the small—the atom—the smallest component of matter. But as it turns out, the atom is **not** matter at all—it is energy—composed of an electrically charged (+) positive proton, an electrically neutral neutron, and an electrically (-) negative electron spinning around the nucleus (protons and neutrons) in an electromagnetic field.

Therefore, an atom is **not** a material reality—it is not physical—it is instead an "invisible" electromagnetic field.

If you combine trillions of these invisible electromagnetic fields (atoms) with diverse atomic structures in the right combinations, you will have a grain of sand. If you combine trillions upon trillions to the trillionth power and more of invisible electromagnetic fields (atoms) with diverse atomic structures in the right combinations, you will have your fleshly body, a tree, a skyscraper, and the universe.

In other words, the present perceived physical universe is made out of nothing but "invisible" electromagnetic fields (atoms). Filippenko and Pasachoff with the Astronomical Society of the Pacific expound on this in *A Universe from Nothing*:

> It is remarkable that the universe consists of essentially nothing, but, fortunately for us, in positive and negative parts. . . . What produced the energy? This is perhaps the ultimate question.[1]

Recognizing, as Filippenko and Pasachoff affirm, that energy is sustaining the present physical universe which is made of nothing but invisible electromagnetic fields, how then does earth and heaven quickly disappear so a new earth and a new heaven can be created?

Quantum physics provides an answer. Quantum physicists assert that an electromagnetic field, an atom, "must have at least one quantum of energy, which means nothing can ever be completely at rest."[2] Consequently, if the energy sustaining the present physical universe is divinely disconnected, what would happen? The universe would collapse into nothing.

Take, for example, a car battery. When cables are connected to (+) positive and (-) negative terminals of a car battery enough energy is discharged to start an engine. But if the (+) positive cable is disconnected no energy can be released and nothing can be produced.

Likewise, if energy is divinely disconnected from the (+) positive protons of invisible electromagnetic fields (atoms), all matter will collapse into nothing and will quickly disappear! As apostle John foretold in Revelation 20:11, "Earth and heaven fled away (Gk., *ephugen* from *pheugo*; vanished suddenly, fled away, **quickly disappeared**)."

Consequently, earth and the entire physical universe that was created from nothing but invisible electromagnetic fields will return to nothing as the temporal gives way to the eternal. Even heaven, God's dwelling, will return to nothing. Early church theologian Tertullian explains:

> The belief that everything was made from nothing will be impressed upon us by that ultimate dispensation of God which will bring back all things to nothing. . . . It shall come to nothing along with the earth itself, with which it was made in the beginning. "Heaven and earth shall pass away," [Matthew 24:35] says He. "The first heaven and the first earth passed away," [Revelation 21:1] "and there was found no place for them [Revelation 20:11]."[3]

Afterwards, dark, matterless outer space. Against this backdrop of infinite darkness will sit the Almighty Jesus Christ, for many the rejected Savior but for everyone the Judge of all mankind, on a great white throne.

## THE GREAT WHITE THRONE JUDGMENT

Earthbound, we tend to imagine the great white throne final judgment as occurring out on a broad plain of the earth. But with all humanity numbering billions of people, and with all the holy angelic host attending as observers, this is hardly a realistic location. Yet, after the universe has vanished, leaving nothing but dark empty outer space, there will be ample accommodation on both sides of the great white throne.

Jesus told us that at the great white throne judgment He will separate "the sheep from the goats" (Matthew 25:31-46), putting "the sheep on His right" and the goats on His left (v. 33). The sheep represent His holy saints clothed in the righteousness of Jesus, our Savior, while the goats symbolize the ungodly, spiritual dead who rejected Jesus as their Savior and His righteousness and who will be judged according to their deeds. As St. John wrote:

> Then I saw a **great white throne** and Him who sat upon it . . . . And I saw the dead, the great and the small, standing before the throne, and books were opened; and another book was opened, which is the book of life; and the dead were judged

from the things which were written in the books, according to their deeds. And the sea gave up the dead which were in it, and death and Hades gave up the dead which were in them; and they were judged, every one of them according to their deeds. And death and Hades were thrown into the lake of fire. This is the second death, the lake of fire. And if anyone's name was not found written in the book of life, he was thrown into the lake of fire. (Revelation 20:11-15)

Irenaeus comments on the great white throne judgment:

For after the times of the [millennial] kingdom, he [John] says, "I saw a **great white throne**, and Him who sat upon it, from whose face the earth fled away, and the heavens; and there was no more place for them." And he sets forth, too . . . the [final] **judgment**, mentioning "the dead, great and small." "The sea," he says, "gave up the dead which it had in it, and death and hell delivered up the dead that they contained; and the books were opened." Moreover, he says, "the book of life was opened, and the dead were judged out of those things that were written in the books, according to their works; and death and hell were sent into the lake of fire, the second death." Now this is what is called Gehenna, which the Lord styled eternal fire. "And if anyone," it is said, "was not found written in the book of life, he was sent into the lake of fire."[4]

This will be a somber day.

But remember, "'As I live!' declares the Lord God, 'I take no pleasure in the death of the wicked, but rather that the wicked turn from his way and live'" (Ezekiel 33:11). "For God so loved the world that he gave his one and only Son [Jesus], that whoever believes in him shall not perish but have eternal life" (John 3:16 NIV).

No person has to stand on the left side of the great white throne. Rather, you can stand on the right side of the throne as one of Christ's holy saints who is forgiven, saved, and clothed in the righteousness of Christ. Make sure—absolutely sure—today of your salvation.

To be saved, God requires two things of you: First, repentance which means that you're going in one direction away from God and you're willing to turn around and go towards God, renouncing those things that are sinful. As the Bible says, "Repent and return, so that your sins may be wiped away" (Acts 3:19). And second, place your faith in Jesus Christ who paid for your sins on the cross by trusting Him as your Savior and Lord.

You may not understand everything now, but Jesus said "as many as received Him, to them He gave the right to become children of God, even to those who believe in His name" (John 1:12). The Bible also says that "Everyone who calls on the name of the Lord will be saved" (Romans 10:13 NIV).

If you're reading this in an airport or in a shopping mall or in the privacy of your home, you can surrender your life to Jesus Christ right now! You can ask Jesus to come into your life right now to be your Savior and Lord. Don't try to clean up your life first, and then come to Christ. Come just as you are, because Jesus only saves sinners.

To trust Jesus Christ as your Savior and Lord, you can pray a simple prayer like this:

> Lord Jesus, I turn from my sins and I turn to follow You as my Savior and Lord. Please forgive my sins and save me. Thank you, Lord Jesus, for forgiving me and for saving me, and for giving me eternal life with you. Thank you also for loving me enough to lay down your life on the cross to save me. In Your name, the name of Jesus, I pray. Amen.

If you have decided to follow Jesus Christ as your Savior and Lord, be sure to go to church this Sunday and tell the pastor of your decision to follow Jesus Christ. Tell him also that you want to be baptized in obedience to Christ's command and as a public profession of your faith in Jesus (Matthew 28:19).

If you have prayed the sinner's prayer and meant it, you belong to Jesus, and not only are you forgiven, saved, and clothed in Christ's righteousness, someday you will live with Him in a new heaven and on a new earth when Jesus makes "all things new" (Revelation 21:5).

# 18

# ALL THINGS NEW

*And He who sits on the throne said,*
*"Behold, I am making all things new." (Revelation 21:5)*

Kettering said, "People are very open minded about new things—as long as they're exactly like the old ones."[1] That is true in this life . . . not in the next. You will love the way the Lord makes "all things new" (Revelation 21:5).

What will be these new things? Well, on the short list are a new heaven and a new earth, a New Jerusalem, and a new quality of life.

## A NEW HEAVEN AND A NEW EARTH

The Psalmist said, "You [Lord] laid the foundation of the earth, and the heavens are the work of Your hands. They will perish, but You will endure; yes, they will all grow old like a garment; like a cloak You will change them, and they will be changed" (Psalm 102:25-26).

Lactantius also comments: "When the thousand years shall be completed, the world shall be renewed by God, and the heavens shall be folded together."[2]

Indeed, after the thousand years of "Sabbath rest for the people of God" (Hebrews 4:9) and the Gog and Magog War (Revelation 20:7-8), and just *before* the commencement of the great white throne final judgment, the present heaven and earth will disappear and perish (Revelation 20:11).

Once the final judgment has concluded, and only Jesus and His holy angels and holy saints remain with Him, our Lord will create a new heaven and a new earth. St. John was privileged to see a glimpse of it in his heavenly vision:

> Then I saw a new heaven and a new earth; for the first heaven and the first earth passed away, and there is no longer any sea. (Revelation 21:1)

As for the new heaven, there is little said about it in the Scriptures. But the Bible does tell us a few things about the new earth. For instance, it will not have a sea or night. For "there is no longer any sea . . . and there will no longer be any night; and they will not have need of the light of a lamp nor the light of the sun, because the Lord God shall illumine them" (Revelation 21:1; 22:5).

Accordingly, in the new creation there will be no darkness, no lamps, and no sun. Illumination will come from Jesus Christ, "the light of the world; he who follows Me [Jesus] shall not walk in darkness" (John 8:12).

Another thing we know about the new earth is that it will have a new city.

## A NEW JERUSALEM

New Jerusalem on the new earth will not be built with the hands of glorified saints—it will come down from heaven. We cannot even imagine the sights along our walks when at last, the city longed for by saints of the ages, the New Jerusalem descends. John the apostle was privileged to see it:

> I saw the holy city, new Jerusalem, coming down out of heaven from God, made ready as a bride adorned for her husband. . . . It had a great and high wall, with twelve gates, and at the gates twelve angels; and names were written on them, which are the names of the twelve tribes of the sons

of Israel. There were three gates on the east and three gates on the north and three gates on the south and three gates on the west. And the wall of the city had twelve foundation stones, and on them were the twelve names of the twelve apostles of the Lamb. (Revelation 21:2, 12-14)

The divinely designed New Jerusalem will be as beautiful as a bride on her wedding day. And, like guests who are often greeted at weddings, so will saints and holy angels visiting the new city be greeted at its gates by holy angels. But not only will New Jerusalem be beautiful, it will be immense:

The city is laid out as a square, and its length is as great as the width; and he measured the city with the rod, fifteen hundred miles (Gk., twelve thousand stadia); its length and width and height are equal. And he measured its wall, seventy-two yards (Gk., one hundred forty-four cubits), according to human measurements, which are also angelic measurements. (Revelation 21:16-17)

In our gravity-bound physical bodies it is difficult for us to comprehend a city that is fifteen hundred miles high, wide, and long. Yet not only will New Jerusalem be colossal, it will be marvelously constructed:

The material of the wall was jasper; and the city was pure gold, like clear glass. The foundation stones of the city wall were adorned with every kind of precious stone. The first foundation stone was jasper; the second, sapphire; the third, chalcedony; the fourth, emerald; the fifth, sardonyx; the sixth, sardius; the seventh, chrysolite; the eighth, beryl; the ninth, topaz; the tenth, chrysoprase; the eleventh, jacinth; the twelfth, amethyst. And the twelve gates were twelve pearls; each one of the gates was a single pearl. And the street of the city was pure gold, like transparent glass. (Revelation 21:18-21)

Can you imagine walking down a street fifteen hundred miles long that is made of pure gold? Wow! Can you also imagine how beautiful its foundation stones will be that are each made of a different jewel? Israel's King Solomon—believed to be the wealthiest person that has ever lived—lived luxuriously, but all that he possessed does not compare to the grandeur of the New Jerusalem.

Yet the best part about the New Jerusalem is not its beauty or its immensity or its jewels or its grandeur. The best part is that the Holy Trinity—the Father, the Son, and the Holy Spirit—will be there, with us:

> Behold, the tabernacle of God is among men, and He will dwell among them, and they shall be His people, and God Himself will be among them. (Revelation 21:3)

Surrounding the new city will be nations of glorified saints who will walk by the light that shines from New Jerusalem. And when we visit the new city, we will bring our finest gifts, our glory, to present and express our love to God whose throne will be in New Jerusalem:

> And the city has no need of the sun or of the moon to shine on it, for the glory of God has illumined it, and its lamp is the Lamb. The nations will walk by its light, and the kings of the earth will bring their glory into it. . . . Its gates will never be closed. . . . And the throne of God and of the Lamb will be in it, and His bond-servants will serve Him; they will see His face . . . and they will reign forever and ever. (Revelation 21:23-25; 22:3-5)

And while we are in New Jerusalem near the throne of God, we can relax alongside the river of the water of life and under a tree of life that are for our healing:

> Then he showed me a river of the water of life, clear as crystal, coming from the throne of God and of the Lamb, in the middle of its street. On either side of the river was the tree of life, bearing twelve kinds of fruit, yielding its fruit every month; and the leaves of the tree were for the healing of the nations. (Revelation 22:1-2)

Yet, besides enjoying the beauty and grandeur of New Jerusalem, and enjoying new glorified immortal healthy bodies, we will also enjoy a new quality of life.

## A NEW QUALITY OF LIFE

*Your Better Life Index* was created by the Organization for Economic Cooperation and Development (OECD) to support policies that promote quality of life. In OECD's assessment of life satisfaction in thirty-four countries, the number one ranking was earned by Denmark. But as high as the quality of life may be for the Danish, it does not compare with the quality of life that the holy saints and the holy angels will enjoy in the new heaven and on the new earth because:

> ... God Himself will be among them, and He will wipe away every tear from their eyes; and there will no longer be any death; there will no longer be any mourning, or crying, or pain; the first things have passed away. (Revelation 21:3-4)

Wailing at funeral services of dear loved ones will no longer be heard, for there will no longer be any death or mourning or crying. God "will wipe away every tear from our eyes" (v. 22:3).

Also, there will be no more pain. In our physical bodies we may stumble and break a bone and experience pain. But in the new heaven and on the new earth we will no longer have flesh and blood bodies. Instead, we will have bodies like the angels that are not subject to broken bones. As Jesus said, "Those who are considered worthy of taking part in the age to come and in the resurrection from the dead will neither marry nor be given in marriage, and they can no longer die; for they are like the angels" (Luke 20:35-36 NIV).

With bodies like angels, with every tear wiped from our eyes, with exciting visits to New Jerusalem, and with a new quality of life, memories of this present life will fade away. As Isaiah foretold:

> For behold, I create new heavens and a new earth; and the former things will not be remembered or come to mind. (Isaiah 65:17)

**183**

My brother or sister in Christ, the birth pains that will strike before our Lord's return and the rapture of the church will be difficult times. As God's Word says, "in the last days difficult times will come (2 Timothy 3:1).

So, when the foretold days of false Christs, wars and rumors of wars, famines, great earthquakes, plaques, extreme weather, terrors, distress of nations, lawlessness, and the tribulation of Antichrist persecution strikes, you can face these difficult times with courage and good cheer knowing that if you stay faithful to Jesus that you will live with Him forever in a new heaven and on a new earth when He makes all things new. And when by His *Amazing Grace* "we've been there ten thousand years, bright shining as the sun . . . [with] no less days to sing God's praise, than when we'd first begun," the former things of this fallen world will not be remembered or come to mind.

How amazingly simple Bible prophecy is when properly understood as the earliest church fathers interpreted and taught it.

# ACKNOWLEDGMENTS

This book was originally intended to be a defense of the doctrine of the day, pretribulational dispensational premillennialism. However, after researching the Scriptures I realized that this interpretation that I had grown up with has serious problems biblically. Yet, I could not understand how end time events could progress differently. This led me to ask God's guidance. Although nothing happened then, a few days later on a quiet Saturday morning the Holy Spirit revealed to me that the church will go through the tribulation—but not the wrath. When that happened, I rushed to my Bible to research it. As I studied the Scriptures, I found that this was the real sure word of prophecy taught in the Bible. However, I did not know how to communicate this since it conflicted with widely held pretribulationism, so I stopped writing. Years passed until I read an article by my former seminary professor, Dr. Thomas D. Lea, who had written briefly on some of the eschatological teachings of the early church Ante-Nicene fathers. As I read his paper and later researched Ante-Nicene fathers' writings, I discovered what the Holy Spirit had revealed to me about prophecy was taught by the majority of Ante-Nicene fathers during the first three centuries of the Christian faith. Thus, the Holy Spirit's leading has made this book possible, and so this book is dedicated to God the Holy Spirit.

Special thanks to my dear wife, Susan, a beloved Proverbs 31 blessing, for patiently enduring while her husband spent much of his spare time over the years researching and writing this book, for the many hours she has spent performing editing, interior and cover design of the book, and for being a treasured wife and best friend. Special thanks also to our dear and treasured children, Brian and Kelsey, who have encouraged their dad in writing this book.

Thanks to the late and dear Dr. Thomas D. Lea, former Dean of Theology at Southwestern Theological Seminary, for his brief research into some of the eschatological teachings of the Ante-Nicene fathers.

Thanks also to dear Bible study friends who encouraged me to write this book.

# ABOUT THE AUTHOR

Robert enjoyed growing up on a wheat farm in northwest Oklahoma where the wind really did come rushing down the plain. After the sale of the farm, he enjoyed his high school years near the Ouachita Mountains in southeast Oklahoma, and attended college in that state. Of course, he is an avid Sooner fan!

After earning a Bachelor's degree in Business Administration, Robert gained a diverse range of theological training in master's and doctoral programs from four seminaries including Southwestern Theological Seminary and Dallas Theological Seminary.

Robert Franklin, D.Min., had only a minimal interest in eschatology until a friend challenged his belief in an eschatological view widely held today among conservative evangelicals. Subsequently, with the aid of the Holy Spirit and with several years of research and documentation of teachings of the earliest church fathers on prophecy, it made possible his book *Rediscovered Early Church Premillennialism: Teachings of the Earliest Church Fathers on Prophecy*. Dr. Franklin and his wife, Susan, have two children and one German Shepherd.

## HOW TO CONTACT THE AUTHOR

If you have questions about something you read in this book, or about Jesus Christ who loves you and wants to have a personal relationship with you, Dr. Franklin would love to hear from you. Or, to schedule Dr. Franklin to speak at your church or seminar or to participate in an interview, please contact him at:

rfranklinbook@yahoo.com

Like our Facebook page: Facebook.com/EarlyChurchPremillennialism

# BIBLIOGRAPHY

## Introduction

1. BBC News Europe. *Sweden: Wedding Ring 'Found on Carrot' After 16 Years,* Retrieved 31 Dec 2011 from: http://www.bbc.co.uk/news/world-europe-16374283.
2. Chafer, Lewis Sperry. *Systematic Theology, Vol. 4, "Eschatology, Introduction,"* Ch. XIII, p. 257, Kregel Publications, Grand Rapids, MI.
3. Ibid.
4. Crutchfield, Larry V. *The Early Church Fathers and the Foundations of Dispensationalism,* Part II, Retrieved 11 Jan 2005 from http://tyndale.edu/dirn/articles/early2.html
5. Roberts, A., Donaldson, J., & Coxe, A. C. *The Ante-Nicene Fathers Vol. I: Translations of The Writings of the Fathers down to A.D. 325,* American reprint of the Edinburgh edition by A. Roberts and J. Donaldson, revised and chronically arranged with prefaces and notes by A. C. Coxe, Buffalo, 1884–1886

## Chapter 1

1. Wiersbe, W. W. (1997, c1992). *Wiersbe's Expository Outlines on the New Testament,* 430. Wheaton, IL: Victor Books.
2. Irenaeus. *Against Heresies,* Book III, Ch. III, para. 4, *The Ante-Nicene Fathers Vol. I: Translations of the Writings of the Fathers down to A.D. 325,* by A. Roberts & J. Donaldson, notes by A. C. Coxe, American reprint of Edinburgh Ed., Eerdmans, Grand Rapids, MI 1884–1886.
3. Irenaeus. *Against Heresies,* Book III, Ch. III, para. 3, *The Ante-Nicene Fathers Vol. I: Translations of the Writings of the Fathers down to A.D. 325,* by A. Roberts & J. Donaldson, notes by A. C. Coxe, American reprint of Edinburgh Ed., Eerdmans, Grand Rapids, MI 1884–1886.
4. Tertullian. *The Prescription Against Heretics,* Ch. XXXII, *The Ante-Nicene Fathers Vol. III: Translations of the Writings of the Fathers down to A.D. 325,* by A. Roberts & J. Donaldson, notes by A. C. Coxe, American reprint of Edinburgh Ed., Eerdmans, Grand Rapids, MI 1884–1886.
5. D'Ambrosio, M. *Early church Fathers Overview: A Snapshot of the Fathers of the church,* Crossroads Productions, Flower Mound, TX, Retrieved: 20 Dec 2010, http://www.crossroadsinitiative.com/library_article/52/Ante-Nicene_church_Fathers_Overview__Snapshot_of_the_Fathers_of_the_church.html.

## Chapter 2

1. Allen, Matthew. *Theology Adrift: The Early church Fathers and Their Views of Eschatology*, Retrieved 7 Sept 2012 from: http://bible.org/article/theology-adrift-early-church-fathers-and-their-views-eschatology.
2. Chafer, Lewis Sperry. *Systematic Theology*, Vol. 4, "Eschatology, Introduction," Ch. XIII, p. 257, Kregel Publications, Grand Rapids, MI.
3. Schaff, Philip. *History of the Christian church*, VIII vols. (Grand Rapids. Eerdmans, 1973), Vol. II, p. 614.
4. Roberts, A., Donaldson, J., Coxe, A.C. *The Ante-Nicene Fathers Vol. I: Translations of the Writings of the Fathers down to AD 325*, "Introductory Note to the Fragments of Papias," American reprint of Edinburgh Ed., Eerdmans, Grand Rapids, MI 1884–1886.
5. *Fragments of Papias*, Ch. VI, *The Ante-Nicene Fathers Vol. I: Translations of the Writings of the Fathers down to A.D. 325*, by A. Roberts & J. Donaldson, notes by A. C. Coxe, American reprint of Edinburgh Ed., Eerdmans, Grand Rapids, MI 1884–1886.
6. Justin Martyr, *Dialogue of Justin*, Ch. LXXXI, *The Ante-Nicene Fathers Vol. I: Translations of the Writings of the Fathers down to A.D. 325*, by A. Roberts & J. Donaldson, notes by A. C. Coxe, American reprint of Edinburgh Ed., Eerdmans, Grand Rapids, MI 1884–1886.
7. Irenaeus. *Against Heresies*, Book V, Ch. XXX, para. 4, *The Ante-Nicene Fathers Vol. I: Translations of the Writings of the Fathers down to A.D. 325*, by A. Roberts & J. Donaldson, notes by A. C. Coxe, American reprint of Edinburgh Ed., Eerdmans, Grand Rapids, MI 1884–1886.
8. St. Jerome. *Chron.*, 2333.
9. Roberts, A., Donaldson, J., Coxe, A.C. *The Ante-Nicene Fathers Vol. V: Translations of the Writings of the Fathers down to AD 325*, "Introductory Notice to Hippolytus," American reprint of Edinburgh Ed., Eerdmans, Grand Rapids, MI 1884–1886.
10. Hippolytus. "The Extant Works and Fragments of Hippolytus, Part I. Exegetical. Fragments from Commentaries on Various Books of Scripture, On Daniel," Ch. II, *The Ante-Nicene Fathers Vol. V: Translations of the Writings of the Fathers down to A.D. 325*, by A. Roberts & J. Donaldson, notes by A. C. Coxe, American reprint of Edinburgh Ed., Eerdmans, Grand Rapids, MI 1884–1886.
11. Roberts, A., Donaldson, J., Coxe, A.C. *The Ante-Nicene Fathers Vol. V: Translations of the Writings of the Fathers down to AD 325*, "Introductory Notice to Hippolytus," American reprint of Edinburgh Ed., Eerdmans, Grand Rapids, MI 1884–1886.
12. Douglas, J. D., Comfort, P. W., & Mitchell, D. (1997, c1992). *Who's Who in Christian History*. Illustrated lining papers. Wheaton, Ill.: Tyndale House.
13. Tertullian. "The Five Books Against Marcion," Book III, Ch. XXV, *The Ante-Nicene Fathers Vol. III: Translations of the Writings of the Fathers down to A.D. 325*, by A. Roberts & J. Donaldson, notes by A. C. Coxe, American reprint of Edinburgh Ed., Eerdmans, Grand Rapids, MI 1884–1886.

14. Victorinus. "On the Creation of the World," *The Ante-Nicene Fathers Vol. VII: Translations of the Writings of the Fathers down to A.D. 325*, by A. Roberts & J. Donaldson, notes by A. C. Coxe, American reprint of Edinburgh Ed., Eerdmans, Grand Rapids, MI 1884–1886.
15. Lactantius. "On a Happy Life," Book VII, Ch. XXVI, *The Ante-Nicene Fathers Vol. VII: Translations of the Writings of the Fathers down to A.D. 325*, by A. Roberts & J. Donaldson, notes by A. C. Coxe, American reprint of Edinburgh Ed., Eerdmans, Grand Rapids, MI 1884–1886.

## Chapter 3

1. New World Encyclopedia, *Millennialism*, Retrieved 14 Dec 2011 from: http://www.newworldencyclopedia.org/entry/Millennialism; (Calvin, John. *The Institutes of the Christian Religion*, Book III, Ch. 25, Section 5).
2. Wikipedia. *Michael Servetus*, Retrieved 14 Dec 2011 from: http://en.wikipedia.org/wiki/Michael_Servetus.
3. Chafer, Lewis Sperry. *Systematic Theology*, Vol. 4, "Eschatology, Introduction," Ch. XIII, p. 257, Kregel Publications, Grand Rapids, MI.

## Chapter 4

1. Riddlebarger, Kim. The Riddleblog, *John MacArthur on Calvinism, Dispensationalism, Israel and Hermeneutics: A Few Comments*, 2011. Site: http://kimriddlebarger.squarespace.com/a-reply-to-john-macarthur/.
2. Carson, D. A. (1994). *New Bible Commentary: 21st century edition*. Rev. ed. of: The New Bible Commentary. 3rd ed. / edited by D. Guthrie, J.A. Motyer. 1970. (4th ed.) (Ge 3:9). Leicester, England; Downers Grove, Ill., USA: Inter-Varsity Press.
3. Ibid.
4. Pike, Ted. *Christians in Israel: An Endangered Species*, National Prayer Network, Retrieved 19 Oct 2012 from: http://www.truthtellers.org/alerts/christiansinisraelrepost.html
5. Strong, A. H. (1907). *Systematic theology* (887). Philadelphia: American Baptist Publication Society.
6. Douglas, J. D., Comfort, P. W., & Mitchell, D. (1997, c1992). *Who's Who in Christian History*. Illustrated lining papers. Wheaton, Ill.: Tyndale House.
7. Justin Martyr. *Dialogue of Justin*, Ch. XI, *The Ante-Nicene Fathers Vol. I: Translations of the Writings of the Fathers down to A.D. 325*, by A. Roberts & J. Donaldson, notes by A. C. Coxe, American reprint of Edinburgh Ed., Eerdmans, Grand Rapids, MI 1884–1886.
8. Tertullian. *On the Resurrection of the Flesh*, Ch. XXII, *The Ante-Nicene Fathers Vol. III: Translations of the Writings of the Fathers down to A.D. 325*, by A. Roberts & J. Donaldson, notes by A. C. Coxe, American reprint of Edinburgh Ed., Eerdmans, Grand Rapids, MI 1884–1886.
9. Tertullian. *An Answer to the Jews*, Ch. III, *The Ante-Nicene Fathers Vol. III: Translations of the Writings of the Fathers down to A.D. 325*, by A. Roberts

& J. Donaldson, notes by A. C. Coxe, American reprint of Edinburgh Ed., Eerdmans, Grand Rapids, MI 1884–1886.


## Chapter 5

1. Hippolytus, "Appendix to the Works of Hippolytus," Ch. XXV, *The Ante-Nicene Fathers Vol. V: Translations of the Writings of the Fathers down to A.D. 325*, by A. Roberts & J. Donaldson, notes by A. C. Coxe, American reprint of Edinburgh Ed., Eerdmans, Grand Rapids, MI 1884–1886
2. Africanus, Julius. "The Extant Fragments of the Five Books of the Chronography of Julius Africanus," Book III, Ch. XVI, *The Ante-Nicene Fathers Vol. VI: Translations of the Writings of the Fathers down to A.D. 325*, by A. Roberts & J. Donaldson, notes by A. C. Coxe, American reprint of Edinburgh Ed., Eerdmans, Grand Rapids, MI 1884–1886.
3. Keil, C. F., & Delitzsch, F. (2002). *Commentary on the Old Testament.* (9:751-763). Peabody, MA: Hendrickson.
4. Miller, S. R. (2001, c1994). "Vol. 18: Daniel." Includes indexes. (electronic ed.). Logos Library System; *The New American Commentary* (239). Nashville: Broadman & Holman Publishers.
5. Keil, C. F., & Delitzsch, F. (2002). *Commentary on the Old Testament.* (9:751-763). Peabody, MA: Hendrickson.
6. Eyewitness to History. *The Romans Destroy the Temple at Jerusalem, 70 AD*, Retrieved 26 Jan 2013 from: http://www.eyewitnesstohistory.com/jewishtemple.htm.
7. Irenaeus, "Against Heresies," Book V, Ch. XXV, para. 4, *The Ante-Nicene Fathers Vol. I: Translations of the Writings of the Fathers down to A.D. 325*, by A. Roberts & J. Donaldson, notes by A. C. Coxe, American reprint of Edinburgh Ed., Eerdmans, Grand Rapids, MI 1884–1886.


## Chapter 6

1. Zodhiates, S. (2000, c1992, c1993). *The Complete Word Study Dictionary: New Testament* (electronic ed.) (G2347). Chattanooga, TN: AMG Publishers.
2. Hippolytus. "The Extant Works and Fragments of Hippolytus, Part II. Dogmatical and Historical, Treatise on Christ and the Antichrist," para. 60," *The Ante-Nicene Fathers Vol. V: Translations of the Writings of the Fathers down to A.D. 325*, by A. Roberts & J. Donaldson, notes by A. C. Coxe, American reprint of Edinburgh Ed., Eerdmans, Grand Rapids, MI 1884–1886.
3. Scofield, C. I. *Prophecy Made Plain: "Addresses on Prophecy"*, Grand Rapids Book Manufacturers, Grand Rapids, MI (1967), p. 130,132.
4. Hippolytus. "The Extant Works and Fragments of Hippolytus, Part II. Dogmatical and Historical, Treatise on Christ and the Antichrist," para. 60," *The Ante-Nicene Fathers Vol. V: Translations of the Writings of the Fathers down to A.D. 325*, by A. Roberts & J. Donaldson, notes by A. C. Coxe, American reprint of Edinburgh Ed., Eerdmans, Grand Rapids, MI 1884–1886.
5. Irenaeus, "Against Heresies," Book V, Ch. XXV, *The Ante-Nicene Fathers Vol. I: Translations of the Writings of the Fathers down to A.D. 325*, by A. Roberts & J. Donaldson, notes by A. C. Coxe, American reprint of Edinburgh Ed., Eerdmans, Grand Rapids, MI 1884–1886.

6.  Hippolytus. "The Extant Works and Fragments of Hippolytus, Part I. Ex-egetical. Fragments from Commentaries on Various Books of Scripture, On Daniel," Ch. II, para. 43, *The Ante-Nicene Fathers Vol. V: Translations of the Writings of the Fathers down to A.D. 325*, by A. Roberts & J. Donaldson, notes by A. C. Coxe, American reprint of Edinburgh Ed., Eerdmans, Grand Rapids, MI 1884–1886.

7.  Tatian. "The Diatessaron of Tatian," Section XLII, *The Ante-Nicene Fathers Vol. X: Translations of the Writings of the Fathers down to A.D. 325*, by A. Roberts & J. Donaldson, notes by A. C. Coxe, American reprint of Edin-burgh Ed., Eerdmans, Grand Rapids, MI 1884–1886.

8.  Hippolytus. "The Extant Works and Fragments of Hippolytus, Part I. Ex-egetical. Fragments from Commentaries on Various Books of Scripture, On Daniel," Ch. II, para. 43, *The Ante-Nicene Fathers Vol. V: Translations of the Writings of the Fathers down to A.D. 325*, by A. Roberts & J. Donaldson, notes by A. C. Coxe, American reprint of Edinburgh Ed., Eerdmans, Grand Rapids, MI 1884–1886.

9.  Irenaeus, "Against Heresies," Book V, Ch. XXV, *The Ante-Nicene Fathers Vol. I: Translations of the Writings of the Fathers down to A.D. 325*, by A. Roberts & J. Donaldson, notes by A. C. Coxe, American reprint of Edin-burgh Ed., Eerdmans, Grand Rapids, MI 1884–1886.

10. Hippolytus. "The Extant Works and Fragments of Hippolytus, Part II. Dogmatical and Historical, Treatise on Christ and the Antichrist," para. 60," *The Ante-Nicene Fathers Vol. V: Translations of the Writings of the Fathers down to A.D. 325*, by A. Roberts & J. Donaldson, notes by A. C. Coxe, American reprint of Edinburgh Ed., Eerdmans, Grand Rapids, MI 1884–1886.

## Chapter 7

1.  Clement of Rome. "First Epistle of Clement to the Corinthians," Ch. XXIII, *The Ante-Nicene Fathers Vol. I: Translations of the Writings of the Fathers down to A.D. 325*, by A. Roberts & J. Donaldson, notes by A. C. Coxe, American reprint of Edinburgh Ed., Eerdmans, Grand Rapids, MI 1884–1886.

2.  Cyprian. "The Treatises of Cyprian, Treatise VII. On the Mortality, para. 2, *The Ante-Nicene Fathers Vol. V: Translations of the Writings of the Fathers down to A.D. 325*, by A. Roberts & J. Donaldson, notes by A. C. Coxe, American reprint of Edinburgh Ed., Eerdmans, Grand Rapids, MI 1884–1886.

3.  Tertullian. "On the Resurrection of the Flesh," Ch. XXII, *The Ante-Nicene Fathers Vol. III: Translations of the Writings of the Fathers down to A.D. 325*, by A. Roberts & J. Donaldson, notes by A. C. Coxe, American reprint of Edinburgh Ed., Eerdmans, Grand Rapids, MI 1884–1886.

4.  Lea, Thomas D. *A Survey of the Doctrine of the Return of Christ in the Ante-Nicene Fathers*, (Journal of the Evangelical Theological Society) June 1986, p. 166-167.

5.

6.  Engelsma, David J. *A Defense of Reformed Amillennialism*, Retrieved 8 Feb 2011 from: http://www.prca.org/articles/amillennialism.html#No5.

7. Ibid.
8. Ibid.

**Chapter 8**

1. Toews, J. E. (2004). *Romans*. Believers church Bible Commentary (223–224). Scottdale, PA: Herald Press.
2. Campbell, I. D. (2008). *Opening up Matthew*. Opening Up Commentary (145–146). Leominster: Day One Publications.
3. Sky News. *Former IT Specialist Claims to be Jesus Reborn*, by Jonathan Samuels, Australia correspondent. Retrieved 14 June 2013 from: http://news.sky.com/story/1096687/former-it-specialist-claims-to-be-jesus-reborn.
4. Tatian. "The Diatessaron of Tatian," Section XLII, *The Ante-Nicene Fathers Vol. X: Translations of the Writings of the Fathers down to A.D. 325*, by A. Roberts & J. Donaldson, notes by A. C. Coxe, American reprint of Edinburgh Ed., Eerdmans, Grand Rapids, MI 1884–1886.
5. Victorinus. "Commentary on the Apocalypse of the Blessed John," From the Sixth Chapter, *The Ante-Nicene Fathers Vol. VII: Translations of the Writings of the Fathers down to A.D. 325*, by A. Roberts & J. Donaldson, notes by A. C. Coxe, American reprint of Edinburgh Ed., Eerdmans, Grand Rapids, MI 1884–1886.
6. Wikipedia. *Great Famine of 1315–1317*, Retrieved 14 June 2013 from: http://en.wikipedia.org/wiki/Great_Famine_of_1315-1317.
7. Ibid.
8. Wikipedia. *Famine*, Retrieved 14 June 2013 from: http://en.wikipedia.org/wiki/Famine.
9. The Real Truth. *Drought Now . . . Famine Next?* Retrieved 28 Apr 2013 from: http://realtruth.org/articles/120815-003.html.
10. Victorinus. "Commentary on the Apocalypse of the Blessed John," From the Sixth Chapter, *The Ante-Nicene Fathers Vol. VII: Translations of the Writings of the Fathers down to A.D. 325*, by A. Roberts & J. Donaldson, notes by A. C. Coxe, American reprint of Edinburgh Ed., Eerdmans, Grand Rapids, MI 1884–1886.
11. Webb, R. *Earthquakes — What are the Long Term Trends*, Retrieved 29 Apr 2013 from: http://www.earth.webecs.co.uk/.
12. Ibid.
13. Hippolytus. "Appendix to the Works of Hippolytus," Ch. VIII, *The Ante-Nicene Fathers Vol. V: Translations of the Writings of the Fathers down to A.D. 325*, by A. Roberts & J. Donaldson, notes by A. C. Coxe, American reprint of Edinburgh Ed., Eerdmans, Grand Rapids, MI 1884–1886.
14. Cyprian. "The Treatises of Cyprian, Treatise VII. On the Mortality, para. 2, *The Ante-Nicene Fathers Vol. V: Translations of the Writings of the Fathers down to A.D. 325*, by A. Roberts & J. Donaldson, notes by A. C. Coxe, American reprint of Edinburgh Ed., Eerdmans, Grand Rapids, MI 1884–1886.
15. Ryan K.J., Ray C.G. (editors) (2004). *Sherris Medical Microbiology* (4th ed.). McGraw Hill. pp. 484–488; Retrieved from: Wikipedia. *Yersina pestis*, on 20 Apr 2013 from: http://en.wikipedia.org/wiki/Yersinia_pestis.
16. History. *Black Death*, A&E Television Networks, LLC, Retrieved 30 Apr

2013 from: http://www.history.com/topics/black-death.

17. Philipkoski, Kristen. *Black Death's Gene Code Cracked*, Wired.com. Retrieved 30 Apr 2013 from: http://www.wired.com/medtech/health/news/2001/10/47288.

18. Hippolytus. "Appendix to the Works of Hippolytus," Ch. VIII, *The Ante-Nicene Fathers Vol. V: Translations of the Writings of the Fathers down to A.D. 325*, by A. Roberts & J. Donaldson, notes by A. C. Coxe, American reprint of Edinburgh Ed., Eerdmans, Grand Rapids, MI 1884–1886.

19. The New York Times. *Heat, Flood or Icy Cold, Extreme Weather Rages Worldwide*, Retrieved 13 May 2013 from: http://www.nytimes.com/2013/01/11/science/earth/extreme-weather-grows-in-frequency-and-intensity-around-world.html?pagewanted=all&_r=0.

20. Ibid.

21. The Weather Channel. *Widest Tornado in History*, Retrieved 5 June 2013 from: http://www.weather.com/video/experts-on-record-widest-tornado-37144.

22. The Weather Channel. *Worst Flooding in Five Centuries*, Retrieved 5 June 2013 from: http://www.weather.com/video/worst-flooding-in-five-centuries-37138.

23. GlobalPost, *Here's the Mountain of Evidence Linking Climate Change to Bigger Storms*, Retrieved 13 May 2013 from: http://www.globalpost.com/dispatch/news/science/global-warming/121030/hurricane-sandy-climate-change-global-warming.

24. Hippolytus. "Appendix to the Works of Hippolytus," Ch. VIII, *The Ante-Nicene Fathers Vol. V: Translations of the Writings of the Fathers down to A.D. 325*, by A. Roberts & J. Donaldson, notes by A. C. Coxe, American reprint of Edinburgh Ed., Eerdmans, Grand Rapids, MI 1884–1886.

25. Wikipedia. *Chelyabinsk Meteor*, Retrieved 11 May 2013 from: http://en.wikipedia.org/wiki/Chelyabinsk_meteor

26. Marshall, I. Howard: *The Gospel of Luke: A Commentary on the Greek Text*. Exeter [Eng.:Paternoster Press, 1978 (The New International Greek Testament Commentary), S. 765.

27. Achtemeier, P. J., Harper & Row, & Society of Biblical Literature. (1985). *Harper's Bible dictionary* (1st ed.) (991). San Francisco: Harper & Row.

28. Spence-Jones, H. D. M. (Hrsg.): *The Pulpit Commentary: St Luke Vol. II*. Bellingham, WA : Logos Research Systems, Inc., 2004, S. 194.

29. Opishposh.com. *The Ten Most Dangerous Countries in 2013*, Retrieved 9 May 2013 from: http://opishposh.com/the-10-most-dangerous-countries/.

30. Realestate.msn.com. *America's Top 5 Most Dangerous Cities*, Retrieved 11 May 2013 from: http://realestate.msn.com/article.aspx?cp-documentid=19959696.

31. New York Post. *Postal Workers too Scared to Deliver Mail in Crime-Ridden Brownsville, Brooklyn*, retrieved 9 May 2013 from: http://www.nypost.com/p/news/local/brooklyn/mailmen_deliver_us_from_evil_9TJh9RgtiTv1FGwOw05MOI.

32. Orwall, Mark. Travel+Leisure, *The World's Most Dangerous Countries*, article June 2009, Retrieved 9 May 2013 from: http://www.travelandleisure.com/articles/the-worlds-most-dangerous-countries

## Chapter 9

1. Hippolytus. "Extant Works, Part II. Dogmatical and Historical, Treatise on Christ and the Antichrist," para. 60," *The Ante-Nicene Fathers Vol. V: Translations of the Writings of the Fathers down to A.D. 325*, by A. Roberts & J. Donaldson, notes by A. C. Coxe, American reprint of Edinburgh Ed., Eerdmans, Grand Rapids, MI 1884–1886.

2. Zodhiates, S. (2000). *The Complete Word Study Dictionary: New Testament* (electronic ed.). Chattanooga, TN: AMG Publishers.

3. *New Bible Commentary: 21st century edition*. 1994 (D. A. Carson, R. T. France, J. A. Motyer & G. J. Wenham, Ed.) (4th ed.) (Re 14:6–20). Leicester, England; Downers Grove, IL: Inter-Varsity Press.

4. Hippolytus. "Extant Works, Part II. Dogmatical and Historical, Treatise on Christ and the Antichrist," para. 60," *The Ante-Nicene Fathers Vol. V: Translations of the Writings of the Fathers down to A.D. 325*, by A. Roberts & J. Donaldson, notes by A. C. Coxe, American reprint of Edinburgh Ed., Eerdmans, Grand Rapids, MI 1884–1886.

5. Schilling, Chelsea. Mayor: Arrested Christians 'Attacked' Michigan City, World Net Daily, Retrieved 21 May 2013 from: http://www.wnd.com/2010/07/178293/.

6. Ibrahim, Raymond. *Crucified Again: Exposing Islam's New War on Christians*, published by Foxnews.com, *The Mass Exodus of Christians from the Muslim World*, retrieved 18 May 2013 from: http://www.foxnews.com/opinion/2013/05/07/mass-exodus-christians-from-muslim-world/.

7. Oleszczuk, Luiza. *Christianity Today India*, retrieved 18 May 2013 from: http://in.christiantoday.com/articles/christians-could-disappear-from-iraq-and-afghanistan/6919.htm.

8. Ibrahim, Raymond. *Crucified Again: Exposing Islam's New War on Christians*, published by Foxnews.com, *The Mass Exodus of Christians from the Muslim World*, retrieved 18 May 2013 from: http://www.foxnews.com/opinion/2013/05/07/mass-exodus-christians-from-muslim-world/.

9. Brewer, Heather. Goodreads.com, Retrieved 21 May 2013 from: http://www.goodreads.com/author/show/293603.Heather_Brewer.

10. Ibrahim, Raymond. *Crucified Again: Exposing Islam's New War on Christians*, published by Foxnews.com, *The Mass Exodus of Christians from the Muslim World*, retrieved 18 May 2013 from: http://www.foxnews.com/opinion/2013/05/07/mass-exodus-christians-from-muslim-world/.

11. Ibid.

12. Wikipedia, *Russian Orthodox church*, http://en.wikipedia.org/wiki/Russian_Orthodox_church.

13. Carson, D. A. (1994). *New Bible Commentary*: 21st century edition. Rev. ed. of: The new Bible commentary. 3rd ed. / edited by D. Guthrie, J.A. Motyer. 1970. (4th ed.) (Re 13:1). Leicester, England; Downers Grove, Ill., USA: Inter-Varsity Press.

14. Beale, G. K. (1999). The book of Revelation: A Commentary on the Greek Text (715). Grand Rapids, Mich.; Carlisle, Cumbria: W.B. Eerdmans; Paternoster Press.

15. Wikipedia, *Cyprian*, Retrieved 24 May 2013 from: http://en.wikipedia.org/

wiki/Cyprian.

16. Cyprian. "Treatise IV. On the Lord's Prayer," para. 13, *The Ante-Nicene Fathers Vol. V: Translations of the Writings of the Fathers down to A.D. 325*, by A. Roberts & J. Donaldson, notes by A. C. Coxe, American reprint of Edinburgh Ed., Eerdmans, Grand Rapids, MI 1884–1886.

17. Hippolytus. "Extant Works, Part II. Dogmatical and Historical, Treatise on Christ and the Antichrist," para. 64," *The Ante-Nicene Fathers Vol. V: Translations of the Writings of the Fathers down to A.D. 325*, by A. Roberts & J. Donaldson, notes by A. C. Coxe, American reprint of Edinburgh Ed., Eerdmans, Grand Rapids, MI 1884–1886.

18. Hippolytus. "Extant Works, Part I. Exegetical, On Daniel," para. 40," *The Ante-Nicene Fathers Vol. V: Translations of the Writings of the Fathers down to A.D. 325*, by A. Roberts & J. Donaldson, notes by A. C. Coxe, American reprint of Edinburgh Ed., Eerdmans, Grand Rapids, MI 1884–1886.

19. Ibid., para. 44.

20. Carson, D. A. (1994). *New Bible Commentary*: 21st century edition. Rev. ed. of: The new Bible commentary. 3rd ed. / edited by D. Guthrie, J.A. Motyer. 1970. (4th ed.) (Re 13:1). Leicester, England; Downers Grove, Ill., USA: Inter-Varsity Press.

21. Richards, L. O. (1991). *The Bible reader's companion* (electronic ed.) (920). Wheaton: Victor Books.

## Chapter 10

1. Elwell, Walter A.; Beitzel, Barry J.: *Baker Encyclopedia of the Bible*. Grand Rapids, Mich.: Baker Book House, 1988, S. 588.

2. Tertullian. "On the Resurrection of the Flesh," Ch. XXVII, *The Ante-Nicene Fathers Vol. III: Translations of the Writings of the Fathers down to A.D. 325*, by A. Roberts & J. Donaldson, notes by A. C. Coxe, American reprint of Edinburgh Ed., Eerdmans, Grand Rapids, MI 1884–1886.

3. Victorinus. "Commentary on the Apocalypse of the Blessed John," From the Sixth Chapter, *The Ante-Nicene Fathers Vol. VII: Translations of the Writings of the Fathers down to A.D. 325*, by A. Roberts & J. Donaldson, notes by A. C. Coxe, American reprint of Edinburgh Ed., Eerdmans, Grand Rapids, MI 1884–1886.

4. Tertullian. "On the Resurrection of the Flesh," Ch. XLI, *The Ante-Nicene Fathers Vol. III: Translations of the Writings of the Fathers down to A.D. 325*, by A. Roberts & J. Donaldson, notes by A. C. Coxe, American reprint of Edinburgh Ed., Eerdmans, Grand Rapids, MI 1884–1886.

5. Victorinus. "Commentary on the Apocalypse of the Blessed John," From the Sixth Chapter, *The Ante-Nicene Fathers Vol. VII: Translations of the Writings of the Fathers down to A.D. 325*, by A. Roberts & J. Donaldson, notes by A. C. Coxe, American reprint of Edinburgh Ed., Eerdmans, Grand Rapids, MI 1884–1886.

## Chapter 11

1. Wood, D. R. W. (1996, c1982, c1962). *New Bible Dictionary* (1250). Inter-

Varsity Press.

2. Cyprian. "Treatise IX. On the Advantage of Patience," para. 21, *The Ante-Nicene Fathers Vol. V: Translations of the Writings of the Fathers down to A.D. 325*, by A. Roberts & J. Donaldson, notes by A. C. Coxe, American reprint of Edinburgh Ed., Eerdmans, Grand Rapids, MI 1884–1886.

3. Louw, J. P., & Nida, E. A. (1996, c1989). *Greek-English Lexicon of the New Testament: Based on Semantic Domains* (electronic ed. of the 2nd edition.) New York: United Bible societies.

4. Kittel, G., Friedrich, G., & Bromiley, G. W. (1995, c1985). *Theological Dictionary of the New Testament.* Translation of: Theologisches Worterbuch zum Neuen Testament. Grand Rapids, Mich.: W.B. Eerdmans.

5. Victorinus. *Commentary on the Apocalypse of the Blessed John*, From the Fifteenth Chapter, *The Ante-Nicene Fathers Vol. VII: Translations of the Writings of the Fathers down to A.D. 325*, by A. Roberts & J. Donaldson, notes by A. C. Coxe, American reprint of Edinburgh Ed., Eerdmans, Grand Rapids, MI 1884–1886.

6. Victorinus. *Commentary on the Apocalypse of the Blessed John*, From the Sixth Chapter, *The Ante-Nicene Fathers Vol. VII: Translations of the Writings of the Fathers down to A.D. 325*, by A. Roberts & J. Donaldson, notes by A. C. Coxe, American reprint of Edinburgh Ed., Eerdmans, Grand Rapids, MI 1884–1886.

7. Utley, R. J. (2001). *Vol. Volume 12: Hope in Hard Times – The Final Curtain: Revelation.* Study Guide Commentary Series (64–65). Marshall, TX: Bible Lessons International.

8. Walvoord, John F. ; Zuck, Roy B. ; Dallas Theological Seminary: *The Bible Knowledge Commentary : An Exposition of the Scriptures.* Wheaton, IL : Victor Books, 1983-c1985, S. 2:949

9. Jamieson, Robert; Fausset, A. R.; Brown, David: *A Commentary, Critical and Explanatory, on the Old and New Testaments.* Oak Harbor, WA : Logos Research Systems, Inc., 1997, S. Re 7:3

10. Blomberg, Craig L. and Chung, Sung Wook. *A Case for Historic Premillennialism: An Alternative to "Left Behind" Eschatology*, p. 82, Baker Academic, Grand Rapids, MI.

11. Foxe, John. *Fox's Book of Martyrs.*

**Chapter 12**

1. Wikipedia. *List of Highest-Grossing Films*, retrieved 24 Feb 2013 from: http://en.wikipedia.org/wiki/List_of_highest_grossing_films#High-grossing_films_by-year.

2. Wikipedia. *The Day After*, retrieved 24 Feb 2013 from: http://en.wikepdia.org/wiki/The_Day_After.

3. Minucius Felix. "Of the End of the Age, Instructions of Commodianus," Ch. XLIII, *The Ante-Nicene Fathers Vol. IV: Translations of the Writings of the Fathers down to A.D. 325*, by A. Roberts & J. Donaldson, notes by A. C. Coxe, American reprint of Edinburgh Ed., Eerdmans, Grand Rapids, MI 1884–1886.

## Chapter 13

1. Methodius. "From the Discourse on the Resurrection," Part 1, para. VIII, *The Ante-Nicene Fathers Vol. VI: Translations of the Writings of the Fathers down to A.D. 325*, by A. Roberts & J. Donaldson, notes by A. C. Coxe, American reprint of Edinburgh Ed., Eerdmans, Grand Rapids, MI 1884–1886.
2. Ibid.
3. Friberg, T., Friberg, B., & Miller, N. F. (2000). Vol. 4: *Analytical Lexicon of the Greek New Testament. Baker's Greek New Testament Library* (288). Grand Rapids, Mich.: Baker Books.
4. Friberg, T., Friberg, B., & Miller, N. F. (2000). Vol. 4: *Analytical Lexicon of the Greek New Testament. Baker's Greek New Testament Library* (288). Grand Rapids, Mich.: Baker Books.
5. Zodhiates, S. (2000, c1992, c1993). *The Complete Word Study Dictionary: New Testament* (electronic ed.) (G3772). Chattanooga, TN: AMG Publishers.
6. Louw, J. P., & Nida, E. A. (1996, c1989). *Greek-English Lexicon of the New Testament: Based on Semantic Domains* (electronic ed. of the 2nd edition.) (1:489). New York: United Bible societies.
7. Robertson, A. (1919; 2006). *A Grammar of the Greek New Testament in the Light of Historical Research* (408). Logos.
8. Friberg, T., Friberg, B., & Miller, N. F. (2000). Vol. 4: *Analytical Lexicon of the Greek New Testament. Baker's Greek New Testament Library* (357). Grand Rapids, Mich.: Baker Books.
9. Friberg, T., Friberg, B., & Miller, N. F. (2000). Vol. 4: *Analytical Lexicon of the Greek New Testament. Baker's Greek New Testament Library* (250). Grand Rapids, Mich.: Baker Books.
10. Kindersley, Dorling. *Infoplease*, Part of Family Education Network, Retrieved 3 Sept 2011 from: http://www.infoplease.com/dk/science/encyclopedia/elements.html#ESC1023NATELE.
11. Emsley, John. *Nature's Building Blocks: An A-Z Guide to the Elements*, (2002) p. 95. Oxford University Press. Retrieved from Chemicool on 03 Sept 2011 from: http://www.chemicool.com/elements/carbon.html].
12. Ibid.
13. Stewart, Doug. *Discovery of Carbon, "Carbon Element Facts."* Chemicool Periodic Table. Chemicool.com. Retrieved 3 Sept 2011 from: http://www.chemicool.com/elements/carbon.html.
14. Metzger, B. M., & United Bible Societies. (1994). *A Textual Commentary on the Greek New Testament*, second edition a companion volume to the United Bible Societies' Greek New Testament (4th rev. ed.) (636). London; New York: United Bible Societies.
15. Irenaeus. "Against Heresies," Book V, Ch. XXXIII, para. 3, *The Ante-Nicene Fathers Vol. I: Translations of the Writings of the Fathers down to A.D. 325*, by A. Roberts & J. Donaldson, notes by A. C. Coxe, American

reprint of Edinburgh Ed., Eerdmans, Grand Rapids, MI 1884–1886.

## Chapter 14

1. Tatian. "The Diatessaron of Tatian," Section XLII, *The Ante-Nicene Fathers Vol. X: Translations of the Writings of the Fathers down to A.D. 325*, by A. Roberts & J. Donaldson, notes by A. C. Coxe, American reprint of Edinburgh Ed., Eerdmans, Grand Rapids, MI 1884–1886.
2. Hippolytus. "The Extant Works and Fragments of Hippolytus, Part I. Exegetical. Fragments from Commentaries on Various Books of Scripture, On Daniel," Ch. II, para. 43, *The Ante-Nicene Fathers Vol. V: Translations of the Writings of the Fathers down to A.D. 325*, by A. Roberts & J. Donaldson, notes by A. C. Coxe, American reprint of Edinburgh Ed., Eerdmans, Grand Rapids, MI 1884–1886.

## Chapter 15

1. Hippolytus. The Extant Works and Fragments of Hippolytus, Part I. "On Daniel," Ch. II, *The Ante-Nicene Fathers Vol. V: Translations of the Writings of the Fathers down to A.D. 325*, by A. Roberts & J. Donaldson, notes by A. C. Coxe, American reprint of Edinburgh Ed., Eerdmans, Grand Rapids, MI 1884–1886.
2. Victorinus, "On the Creation of the World," *The Ante-Nicene Fathers Vol. VII: Translations of the Writings of the Fathers down to A.D. 325*, by A. Roberts & J. Donaldson, notes by A. C. Coxe, American reprint of Edinburgh Ed., Eerdmans, Grand Rapids, MI 1884–1886.
3. Victorinus, "On the Creation of the World," *The Ante-Nicene Fathers Vol. VII: Translations of the Writings of the Fathers down to A.D. 325*, by A. Roberts & J. Donaldson, notes by A. C. Coxe, American reprint of Edinburgh Ed., Eerdmans, Grand Rapids, MI 1884–1886
4. Ibid.
5. Lactantius. The Divine Institutes, Book VI, "Of a Happy Life," Ch. XIV, *The Ante-Nicene Fathers Vol. VII: Translations of the Writings of the Fathers down to A.D. 325*, by A. Roberts & J. Donaldson, notes by A. C. Coxe, American reprint of Edinburgh Ed., Eerdmans, Grand Rapids, MI 1884–1886.
6. Ibid.
7. Victorinus, "On the Creation of the World," *The Ante-Nicene Fathers Vol. VII: Translations of the Writings of the Fathers down to A.D. 325*, by A. Roberts & J. Donaldson, notes by A. C. Coxe, American reprint of Edinburgh Ed., Eerdmans, Grand Rapids, MI 1884–1886.
8. Lactantius. The Divine Institutes, Book VII, "Of a Happy Life," Ch. XVII, *The Ante-Nicene Fathers Vol. VII: Translations of the Writings of the Fathers down to A.D. 325*, by A. Roberts & J. Donaldson, notes by A. C. Coxe, American reprint of Edinburgh Ed., Eerdmans, Grand Rapids, MI 1884–1886.
9. Papias. "Fragments of Papias," Ch.. IV, *The Ante-Nicene Fathers Vol. I: Translations of the Writings of the Fathers down to A.D. 325*, by A. Roberts & J. Donaldson, notes by A. C. Coxe, American reprint of Edinburgh Ed., Eerdmans, Grand Rapids, MI 1884–1886.

## Chapter 16

1. Lactantius. "The Divine Institutes,, *Of a Happy Life*," Book VII, Ch. XXVI, *The Ante-Nicene Fathers Vol. VII: Translations of the Writings of the Fathers down to A.D. 325*, by A. Roberts & J. Donaldson, notes by A. C. Coxe, American reprint of Edinburgh Ed., Eerdmans, Grand Rapids, MI 1884–1886.
2. Balz, H. R., & Schneider, G. (1990-c1993). *Exegetical Dictionary of the New Testament*. Translation of: *Exegetisches Worterbuch zum Neuen Testament*. (1:267). Grand Rapids, Mich.: Eerdmans.
3. Spence-Jones, H. D. M. (Hrsg.): *The Pulpit Commentary: Ezekiel Vol. II.* Bellingham, WA : Logos Research Systems, Inc., 2004, S. 287.
4. Lactantius. "The Divine Institutes, Book VII, *Of a Happy Life*," Ch. XVII, *The Ante-Nicene Fathers Vol. VII: Translations of the Writings of the Fathers down to A.D. 325*, by A. Roberts & J. Donaldson, notes by A. C. Coxe, American reprint of Edinburgh Ed., Eerdmans, Grand Rapids, MI 1884–1886.

## Chapter 17

1. Filippenko, Alexei V. and Pasachoff, Jay M. Astronomical Society of the Pacific, *A Universe from Nothing*, Retrieved 22 Sept 2011 from: http://www.astrosociety.org/pubs/mercury/31_02/nothing.html.
2. Worsley School. *Quantum Physics*, Retrieved 22 Sept 2011 from: http://www.worsleyschool.net/science/files/quantum/physics.html.
3. Tertullian. "*Against Hermogenes*," Containing an Argument Against His Opinion that Matter is Eternal, Ch. XXXIV, *The Ante-Nicene Fathers Vol. III: Translations of the Writings of the Fathers down to A.D. 325*, by A. Roberts & J. Donaldson, notes by A. C. Coxe, American reprint of Edinburgh Ed., Eerdmans, Grand Rapids, MI 1884–1886.
4. Irenaeus. *Against Heresies*, Book V, Ch. XXXV, *The Ante-Nicene Fathers Vol. I: Translations of the Writings of the Fathers down to A.D. 325*, by A. Roberts & J. Donaldson, notes by A. C. Coxe, American reprint of Edinburgh Ed., Eerdmans, Grand Rapids, MI 1884–1886.

## Chapter 18

1. Kettering, Charles. *Charles Kettering Quotes*, Retrieved 4 April 2013 from: http://www.brainyquote.com/quotes/authors/c/charles_kettering.html.
2. Lactantius. "The Divine Institutes, *Of a Happy Life*, Book VII, Ch. XXVI, *The Ante-Nicene Fathers Vol. VII: Translations of the Writings of the Fathers down to A.D. 325*, by A. Roberts & J. Donaldson, notes by A. C. Coxe, American reprint of Edinburgh Ed., Eerdmans, Grand Rapids, MI 1884–1886.

# NOTES

# NOTES

www.ingramcontent.com/pod-product-compliance
Lightning Source LLC
LaVergne TN
LVHW011156080426
835508LV00007B/437